Halifax Down!

Halifax Down!

On the Run from the Gestapo, 1944

TOM WINGHAM

GRUB STREET · LONDON

Published by
Grub Street Publishing
4 Rainham Close
London
SW11 6SS

Copyright © Grub Street 2009
Copyright text © Tom Wingham 2009

British Library Cataloguing in Publication Data
Wingham. Tom
  Halifax down!: on the run from the Gestapo, 1944.
  1. Wingham, Tom. 2. Escapees – Belgium – History – 20th
  century. 3. World War, 1939-1945 – Personal narratives,
  British. 4. Belgium – History – German occupation, 1940-1945.
  I. Title
  940.5′48141-dc22

ISBN 9781906502393

Typeset by Pearl Graphics, Hemel Hempstead

Printed and bound by the MPG Books Group, Bodmin, Cornwall

Grub Street Publishing uses only FSC (Forest Stewardship Council)
paper for its books

Contents

Foreword

As a teenager in the 1950s, I was an avid reader of the books written by the 'aces' of the Second World War together with those such as the Dam Busters, Great Escape, Colditz and other daring tales of the experiences of RAF aircrew. In recent years, as the Archivist of the Aircrew Association, I have noted a significant increase in the publication of the memoirs and experiences of those I call 'The Many'. Some have been written by families and there are others that go over familiar ground. However, I have been particularly inspired by those that relate the experiences of men shot down behind enemy lines and who avoided capture. They never cease to amaze me. Tom Wingham's inspiring tale falls into that category.

I have known Tom for a number of years and was aware that during the Second World War he had been posted as 'missing' from a bomber operation but had eventually returned to safety. I was much more aware of his devoted work as the secretary of 102 Squadron Association, his old wartime squadron. It was largely due to his efforts that this wartime squadron still meets for annual reunions. I have also developed the greatest admiration for his wonderful work to discover the fate of his colleagues who remain 'missing'. He has traced many of them and identified the circumstances in which they were lost. His work has led to the families discovering the fate of their loved ones and thus being able finally to gain the peace they have wanted as their missing relatives have been laid to rest. Tom's discoveries have also led to a number of memorials being erected by the people of Holland, Belgium and France as a lasting tribute to these brave men.

Tom also has a special affection for these people as readers of this book will discover, and it will soon become apparent why. His modesty had previously prevented him from going into detail of how he evaded capture but in recent years friends and family have prevailed upon him to record his experiences and thank goodness they did.

This is a stimulating story, and how fitting, and typical, that he should follow the fortunes of his crew. The courage, fortitude and resolve of young men who found themselves behind enemy lines always captivates me and my admiration for them knows no bounds. However, Tom would be the first to agree with me that I should also highlight the unbelievable courage of the 'helpers', those ordinary gallant people in enemy-occupied territories who saw it as their duty to help Allied airmen knowing that they could, if discovered, pay the ultimate price for their deeds, as so many did.

The courageous deeds of all these remarkable aircrew and their equally remarkable 'helpers' should live forever and be an inspiration for future generations. This book does just that.

Air Commodore G R Pitchfork, MBE, FRAeS
Gloucestershire

Introduction

On the night of 22/23 April 1944, I was the bomb aimer in the crew of a 76 Squadron Halifax shot down while on the way to bomb Dusseldorf. I was fortunate, together with Jim Lewis, the navigator, to be able to evade capture and after nearly five months on the run, to return home back to RAF service.

After the war, I remained in contact with Jim and, although over the years many a beer was quaffed together, it was very rare for any mention to be made of the time we spent in Holland and Belgium. Apart from one name, I knew nothing of the Dutch people who had helped me out, but, for several years, I maintained correspondence with the Belgians until, following a move, I mislaid all the names and addresses early in the 1950s. Some ten years later I re-discovered the papers in the attic but decided that, perhaps, it was time to let the past bury itself. However, at the end of January 1977 I received a letter out of the blue from Holland, through the RAF Association, in which I was advised that one of my Dutch helpers was dying and his family was hoping that I could visit him. Apparently, of the thirty-nine aircrew he assisted to safety, I was the last and the only one whose name he knew. At the end of March 1977, I met Richard Linckens and his wife Ciska for the first time since they had given me sanctuary thirty-three years previously. Sadly Richard died about six weeks later.

As a result of this visit, I was able to re-establish contact with all those good Dutch and Belgian people who had helped me in 1944 and who still survived. The account of my successful evasion will I trust stand as tribute to their courage.

In 1989 I was contacted by Leo Pierey, a Netherlander who was born and brought up in the vicinity of our crashed aircraft at Gulpen. At the age of eighteen in 1943 he had been taken by the Germans to work as forced labour in Essen but in May 1944 had absconded back to his home to stay in hiding until the liberation of his homeland four months later. Now in 1989 he was assisting a Dutch air historian to write a book on the history of some 380 aircraft which crashed in the Dutch province of Limburg during the war. As a result of his interest I was able to visit the site of our downed aircraft for the first time and, after some effort, contact the other surviving members of the crew, all still alive, although Sid Stephen had emigrated to Australia not many years after the war.

With Leo's help I was able to plot approximately where everyone had landed that night which, combined with each member's story, gave this broad picture of what happened individually to the crew of a heavy bomber after it was hit. Since we lost thousands of heavy bombers during the war this account can, I hope, serve as a sample picture of those losses. I was lucky, being the only member of the crew to walk away without any physical injury and then to have a not unpleasant period evading capture. It was not until the late 1980s that I realised the ordeal that other members of my crew had undergone. The treatment meted out to Jack Reavill was barbaric and much of his account remains untold but I trust that I have been able to record sufficient to show that not all RAF prisoners were held in Stalaglufts where the rules were kept.

It has been fashionable for some historians and intelligentsia to decry the efforts of Bomber Command and of "Butch" Harris in particular. When I first returned to Holland in 1977 I was over-whelmed by the warmth of the welcome I received after so many years and when I protested that it was I who owed the thanks for the help given, this was brushed aside with the words, "the sound of your engines was the only hope we had that the war was still being carried on". In 1992, after the unveiling of the Harris statue with its protest, I received a letter from Leo Pierey from which I quote:

"All over the world there are people who, without shade, judge of affairs they know nothing about. However, with regard to the last war, I think there will be little difference between your and my country as we went through four-five years of terrible occupation. Here the cry, 'Harris was a mass-murderer', will not easily be heard. We have much more the tendency to sanction all that contributed to the fall of the barbarian Nazi power. I myself suffered terrible bombardments during my forced stay in Germany – the last ten months in Essen – but never did the idea cross my mind to condemn the RAF. The British – and later also the Americans – held our only hope for liberation."

Perhaps some future historians may balance the above against their obsession with Dresden.

AVIS

Toute personne du sexe masculin qui aiderait, directement ou indirectement, les équipages d'avions ennemis descendus en parachute, ou ayant fait un atterrissage forcé, favoriserait leur fuite, les cacherait ou leur viendrait en aide de quelque façon que ce soit, sera fusillée sur le champ.

Les femmes qui se rendraient coupables du même délit seront envoyées dans des camps de concentration situés en Allemagne.

Les personnes qui s'empareront d'équipages contraints a atterrir, ou de parachutistes, ou qui auront contribué, par leur attitude, à leur capture, recevront une prime pouvant aller jusqu'à **10.000** francs. Dans certains cas particuliers, cette récompense sera encore augmentée.

Paris, le 22 Septembre 1941.

Le Militärbefehlshaber in Frankreich.
Signé: von **STÜLPNAGEL**
Général d'Infanterie.

Notice displayed widely in all occupied countries.

Translation

Any male person directly or indirectly helping the crew of enemy aircraft landed by parachute or having effected a forced landing, or assisting in their evasion, or hiding and helping them in any way whatever, will be shot immediately.

Women guilty of the same offence will be deported to concentration camps in Germany.

Any persons seizing crew members having effected a forced landing or descended by parachute, or who, by their attitude, contribute to their capture, will receive a reward of up to 10,000 francs. In some cases this reward will be even higher.

Paris, 22 September 1941
The Military Governor of France
Signed: von Stülpnagel
Infantry General

11

The Crew

Halifax MP-I MZ 578

Pilot: Squadron Leader S. Somerscales, DFC

Bomb Aimer: Flying Officer S.T. Wingham

Navigator: Flying Officer J.H. Lewis, DFM

Wireless Operator: Flying Officer J.H. Reavill, DFM

Engineer: Pilot Officer S.W. Stephen

Rear Gunner: ~~Wireless~~ *Warrant* Officer F.J. Rowe

Mid-Upper Air Gunner: Flight Sergeant H.R. Poole

Chapter I

Early Years and Training

"God, it's cold! Where the hell are the bed clothes?" Reaching down to pull the blankets up, my hand just grasped fresh air. "What clot's pinched them?" Somehow the bed seemed harder than usual and my pillow had disappeared as well but at least the b------s had left me with the sheet I was lying on.

Flat on my back I opened my eyes and gradually focused. Above me was the sky, dark but clear, with the stars just a blur. Damn! I obviously was not in my quarters and nobody had taken my bedding. But what was I doing here in the middle of a field? This was the first time I'd ended up like this. However much we drank I had always made it back to quarters before, but then there always has to be a first time!

Everything was so quiet. Not a sound to be heard, not a light to be seen, as I lay there endeavouring to collect my senses. Where had I been last night to end up like this? My mouth didn't taste like I had been on a binge and, anyway, we always tripped into York in Jim's car. But what were these cords doing tangled up around me? Groping around I traced the cords which were not only attached to the sheet but ended up linked to the harness in which I was still strapped. The penny dropped. I was lying on a parachute. But how did I get here?

Even more than fifty years on, those first few minutes as I came to remain vivid in my mind. How long it took while I gathered my senses together I will never know. Trying to read my watch proved impossible as I was unable to focus properly due to what I was later to realise was the effect of concussion. Gradually my mind cleared

and images began to form. Dropping through the forward escape
hatch, seeing the black bulk of the port wing and fuselage above,
pulling the rip-cord, then – nothing, till I woke up on the ground.
The thought that I was in enemy territory had not yet come to mind
as I painfully tried to think back for the reason why I had been on
the end of a parachute. For a while I tried to convince myself I had
baled out over England and all that now had to be done was to find
the nearest phone and contact base, but gradually memory returned.
We hadn't reached the target and I was the wrong side of the
Channel. Panic! Action was necessary! I must hide the 'chute and get
away. But which way? At that moment the question of which
country I was in did not seem relevant. If we had been near the Ruhr
then there was but one direction to go, south-west. In almost one
movement I hit the quick release of the harness, gathered up the
parachute and jumped up to run, only to fall flat on my face in pain.
Bomber Command could not afford the disruption that proper
parachute instruction and practice would bring, with a tally of
sprains and possibly bone fractures among its aircrew, apart from
the cost and the possibility that aircrew might bale out more readily;
there were a few members of the Air Council who were always
obsessed with the chance of morale breaking, so the sum total of
instruction had been a couple of short sessions a long time ago in the
gym on how to collapse when hitting the ground. For the observer
type parachute, which was clipped on to the chest, it was necessary
to fold the arms across the chest to protect from the whip of the
harness straps as the parachute opened. Failure to do that when
baling out had allowed the heavy clips to hit me: two perfect clips to
the jaw, as the chute opened up, so knocking me out. Being
unconscious, I must have landed like a sack of potatoes and my legs
and back had suffered. The heavy clouts from the clips had also
produced the concussion which was now causing blurred vision.

Having learnt the hard way, I again got to my feet, but this time,
more gingerly, keeping my head firmly facing forwards. Moving to
the edge of the field where there was a hedge, I found a small

depression into which I forced down the parachute and harness before covering it up as best as possible, and, as well as could be seen in the blackness of the night. Having got rid of this encumbrance the pressing problem was to get as far away as possible. At this stage my only recollection was of being a few minutes short of the target when the order to bale out had been given, so I could be in Germany, Belgium or Holland, although my reason had not yet returned sufficiently to think through the latter. (I was later to discover that my aircraft crashed near Gulpen only some six miles from the German border). At the time I probably only reacted with animal instinct to turn and run and so, with a navigational training behind me, south-west seemed the most sensible way in which to head.

But where was south-west? As soon as I dropped my head to read the watch on my wrist there was an immediate blurring of vision, so there was no way it was going to be possible to read a compass, particularly in the dark. I looked up for the Pole Star but as soon as my head moved from the normal position the stars became a blur. Nothing else for it. I lowered myself to the ground, lay flat on my back and, centring my head, was able to see all the sky clearly. Selecting the Pole Star I lined my feet up to point south-west then sat up and again looked skyward to identify the shape of the blur where the Pole Star lay. With this as a reference point, I could now aim towards possible safety.

Dazed and aching, I walked on what I hoped was a south-west line regardless of hedges, barbed wire or roads, although I had to skirt round an isolated house where a dog threatened to awake the dead. There were no sign posts to give a clue as to position and eventually I came to a small river. Taking off my flying boots and socks and walking along the bank testing the water, I eventually found a spot to wade across. The river lay in a small depression and was lined with trees on either side. A little way along, the trees were somewhat more numerous on a bend in the river and about four deep, sufficient to give some cover and time to think and rest during the daylight which was now becoming imminent. In my present state there was no way I could do much running if caught in the open, so, lying down on the grassy bank, I dozed and waited for the dawn.

When the sun rose the time came to assess my situation. I was lying on a sloping bank some twenty feet from the edge of the river. Crawling a few feet further away from the bank I raised my head out of the depression and viewed the south-west line that had to be taken. I was confronted by open fields all around me, with no buildings visible except for a church steeple to the south-east. However, in the distance there appeared to be extensive wooded country. The sight of this gave great relief, for my overwhelming desire was to stay out of sight, at least until I could establish where I was. There was no sign of roads or railways and I felt completely alone. Even allowing for the fact that it was Sunday everything was strangely quiet with nothing to indicate any life around me. Even so it seemed advisable to rest for the day to recover my strength and shake off the concussion before moving on.

With the light it was also possible to take stock of my resources by opening up my escape box. This was one of two packs issued to aircrew prior to any operational flight over enemy territory. The other pack contained silk maps covering the areas over which operations were being carried out. Since I had not yet found any prominent landmarks I left these in my pocket and concentrated on the celluloid box some five and half by four and a half inches and three quarters of inch deep, known throughout the RAF as a 'Pandora box'. Much of the space inside the box was absorbed by a rubber water bottle but even so there was room left for a selection of Dutch, Belgian and French notes, water purification tablets, a compass and some Horlicks tablets. Going down to the water's edge I filled the bottle and dropped a purification tablet in just to play safe before breakfasting on very cold water and a Horlicks tablet. Strangely enough, I had no feeling of hunger.

Now I had time to lie back and think about my predicament. Like most aircrew on bomber stations I had sat listening once or twice to escapers who had got back home after baling out but, somehow, it didn't help the feeling of loneliness as I decided what to do next. One thing was certain; when an aircraft crashed the Germans knew how many crew should be in it and would therefore be out and about scouring the area. I wondered how far away the Halifax had come down and whether everyone had got out. Way back in my OTU days, I had taken part in an evasion exercise when we were loaded into a closed lorry after dark and then dumped in open country with the object of getting back to the airfield without being caught by instructors who were placed at strategic points to intercept us. Playing a waiting game, I timed my run so that I was the last one in with just a few minutes to spare, banking on the instructors getting tired of waiting after they had caught the majority. With this in mind it seemed best to hide up in the day and travel at night, at least until I had established where I was. So I made myself as comfortable and as inconspicuous as possible and tried to get some sleep.

During the day I dozed in fits and starts in the quiet of the countryside in which there was no sound of movement, no traffic, no people, no voices; in fact, it seemed almost unreal, a dream. A sign of movement came mid-afternoon. A man, seemingly searching the river bank, began to move towards me albeit very slowly. There was no cover where I sat on the ground and the trees were rather sparse. Picking the thickest tree trunk, which was just about the width of my shoulders, I put it between me and the man, breathed in, and awaited developments. Peering out from behind the tree the reason for the man's slow progress became obvious as he drew towards me. He was fishing the river, casting his line and waiting awhile before reeling in, moving a few paces along the bank and then repeating the process. It must have been nearly an hour from the time he came into view before I was able to heave a sigh of relief with his departure. For a time he was barely twenty feet from me and it was probably the only time in my life I prayed that a man should not catch a fish, in case he wanted to dally further in the waters before me. As he disappeared in the distance, an unseen church bell began to toll, but not from the church that was visible. It came from a nearby monastery (Wittem) which, I was not to know at the time, was the only bell in the area that the Germans had not taken to melt down.

As evening came, I re-filled my water bottle and, with the fall of darkness, began my south-west trek. My knees and back still ached and the concussion was still with me, and indeed was to last for at least two weeks. This blurred vision became a nuisance whenever I moved my head up or down, but I quickly got into the habit of turning my whole body to face up to the direction of view and to lie flat on my back to get a bearing from the Pole Star. As I plodded across the fields this trick had to be performed several times as I lost bearings or diverted to avoid a barking dog. Progress was rather slow but eventually I reached the woods I had viewed from the river and with some relief was able to walk without having to worry about hedges, fences, ditches or dogs. The night was black and with no defined path I wandered through the woods trying to maintain something approaching south-west. Just before dawn, reaching the southern edge of the trees on a hill overlooking a village, I settled down to review the position and await the light.

*   *   *

There is a tendency, when you are in trouble, to look back and contemplate what could have been done to avoid it, however futile the exercise. As I lay in the woods, dozing on and off, it was in such a review that I engaged myself, thinking back over the years that had brought me to this predicament.

Born in the East End of London, I had been brought up during the inter-war years seeing annually the massed RAF squadrons over-flying the capital as they made their way to the great Hendon air shows which were such a feature of life at that time. Nearly all my teachers had fought in the trenches during the Great War and, together with all the illustrated magazines available, had imparted the horror of that sort of warfare. Being an avid reader of W.E. Johns, there was no place I could imagine better, in the event of war, than being in the Royal Air Force. In the second half of the thirties, as I reached my teens and was completing my education, the inevitability of war became a common topic of conversations in classrooms. I was convinced more than ever that, if the time came to fight, I would want to be up and away in the air, free from the mess below.

As the spring of 1939 came I sought to join the RAF as a boy entrant but my mother, persuaded by a non-conformist preacher that "if God wanted us to fly, He would have given us wings", would not give the necessary approval, leaving me no alternative but to wait until war arrived. This duly turned up in September, when I immediately wrote to the Air Ministry offering my services, only to receive a reply suggesting that I should renew the offer when I was eighteen. The next sixteen months dragged by as first we endured the 'phoney war', followed by the fall of France and then the Battle of Britain. Came the Blitz and living in the East End of London I developed a yearning for revenge against the enemy who was smashing down and burning the London I loved and of which I was proud. I was watching the West Ham v. Tottenham match at Upton Park on that Saturday in September 1940 when the Luftwaffe launched their attack upon the London Docks, interrupting the match and sending us home early with the docks aflame.

For a while, during the night-bombing which followed in the autumn of 1940, I would stay with my family doctor at nights to give him some company and man his telephone when he was called out. This came to an end when my mother had to evacuate our house due to a landmine and went to live with her sister, my aunt, in south Croydon. After fending for myself for a week or so I decided to follow. As far as one could see it was a case of out of the frying pan into the fire, literally, since most of the raids came from the south and consequently overflew Croydon. The area received a fair share of the bomb loads which were shed as the bombers ran into the anti-aircraft barrage of the London defences. In spite of the continuous enemy activity throughout that winter of 1940/41 I always somehow managed to sleep soundly in my bed, except for occasional forays into the night to extinguish incendiary bombs and put out fires in neighbouring empty houses. Due to the houses being large and well-spaced out most bombs managed to find open ground.

Promptly on my eighteenth birthday in January 1941 I applied for aircrew duties in the RAF. I naturally opted for pilot and, in due course, reported to Oxford for selection tests and a medical, ending up before a selection panel who decided that I, in their opinion, would be of more value to the Royal Air Force as an observer, (terminology at that time for navigator), rather than flying one of their aircraft. Having taken the Oath of Allegiance and raring to go, it was with much chagrin that the group I was with learnt that our call-up would be deferred for six months until the air force could cope with us. So I returned to Croydon to sit out bombs, guns and shrapnel raining down for another six months, frustrated at not being able to hit back. Eventually, my call-up came with orders to report to the Aircrew Reception Centre at Regent's Park on the 19th July.

The ACRC had only recently been set up in London to handle the flow of trainee aircrew which would be necessary to maintain the efforts of the various RAF Commands. Obviously, even at that time of the war, somebody somewhere had done their sums and worked out an estimated 'chop' rate which we were likely to suffer; but such thoughts did not enter our heads at the time. The centre was based around Lord's cricket ground and London Zoo with many of the surrounding large blocks of flats commandeered, emptied and furnished with service iron bedsteads on which were three stuffed palliasses and blankets. The organization was somewhat stretched in these early days but with the issue of uniforms and everything to accompany them we were allocated to different flights and commenced drill in the streets and park. So we began the process of being tuned to meet the requirements of a modern fighting force.

Although some animals had been removed from the Regent's Park zoo there were still enough left to attract visitors and, as we marched three times a day to the restaurant which was our mess, we became an additional attraction as 'Feeding time at the Zoo' took place. Even in wartime the West End of London still kept its allure and most evenings we were able to wander about thoroughly enjoying the theatres and cinemas in the area. After finishing at midday on Saturdays we were able to go home until Sunday night. The only discordant note was the continuance of night air raids. Having slept through them for nearly a year in my own bed it was, to say the least, annoying to be woken up in the middle of the night by the air raid sirens and the strident voices of the NCOs and compelled, in military fashion, to abandon the comfort of bed for the cold of the basement shelter. Still, it was summer and I was in the RAF, so this had to be endured.

At the end of our allotted spell at ACRC we found ourselves posted on 16th August to various Initial Training Wings and I was fortunate to be sent to No.1 at Babbacombe, just outside Torquay. Classified as U/T (under training) aircrew we all wore white flashes in our forage caps indicating our role as cadets. We were all destined to become officers, either commissioned or non-commissioned and the purpose of ITW was to teach the basics of military discipline and drill to enable us to fulfill the role when the time came.

Babbacombe, being a holiday resort, had many hotels and guest houses along the cliff top, all of which had been commandeered by the air force, and a Hawker Hind parked in front to, presumably, connect us aspiring aviators with a flying machine, however obsolete. For eight weeks we marched and drilled, always at 140 paces per minute, sometimes in uniform, sometimes running along the cliffs in PT gear and, occasionally, wearing gas masks. We learnt basic navigational theory, aircraft recognition, the Morse Code and wireless telegraphy to twelve words per minute, King's regulations and gunnery, in particular, the Vickers gas-operated machine gun, dismantling and assembling the weapon blindfolded. As a sideline, and to learn the rudiments of air gunnery, we were introduced to clay pigeon shooting which, with swimming, provided very welcome breaks from the routine. Of course, this was still a five and a half day week we were working and so, at midday on Saturdays we were free until 'lights out' on Sunday nights to get to know Torquay, the surrounding countryside, and the various sights in the area. Not many of us had been able previously to afford such a long and pleasant vacation.

To add to the sense of holiday we also had the occasional use of a launch out of Torquay harbour for a trip round the bay in order to practice basic navigation using compass bearings off various points. And all this at no charge! Not at the time, anyway. The bill was to be collected sometime in the future. That beautiful summer passed all too quickly with the help as well of a do-it-yourself concert in the pavilion on the cliffs which was organised by one of the flight commanders, a peacetime school master, with amateur theatricals as a hobby. With the short time available for rehearsals it was quite a fair effort. But by 10th October our time was up and, with the exception of one of our number who had failed the course, we were duly passed out, with a promotion from AC2 (aircraftman second class) to LAC (leading aircraftman), and sent off for three weeks embarkation leave. No mention was made of our destination.

Early in November we all reassembled at Babbacombe after our leave and joined up with groups from the other ITWs at Torquay and Brixham. We were issued with travelling rations and packed into a special train awaiting us at the railway station. Wartime train journeys were notoriously bad, but the one on which we embarked descended well below the lowest expectations as, through the late afternoon and night, we visited and occupied for various periods every siding that could be found between Torquay and Liverpool. We eventually de-trained late the following afternoon at a station near to the RAF Embarkation Holding Centre at West Kirby, near Liverpool. It was now 5th November and we began to get an inkling of our destination as we were issued with tropical kit, including pith helmets, as well as undergoing tropical injections, which made it obvious that Canada, the main bet, was not on the itinerary. West Kirby was a bleak windswept camp intended to hold airmen for short periods and consequently entertainment was not a priority, even though we were confined to camp. The high and low spots were the daily parades as names were read out and assigned to different groups, with those not listed watching the others marched away for onward movement. These first few months in uniform had me yearning for a different name as I found everything was carried out in alphabetical order, leaving me, in company with Frank Whittaker, always at the end of the queue. Joy for those listed, disconsolation for those who had to endure another twenty-four hours in this God forsaken spot. But we were lucky. Although it seemed a lifetime, we were posted within a few days.

Again we packed our kitbags, were issued with travelling rations, and on the 10th November embarked for another interminable train journey. Hope had been for a short trip to the Liverpool docks but it was not to be and it was almost midnight when we detrained at Glasgow and boarded the 22,000 ton *Arundel Castle* which was to be our home for the next six weeks. Our quarters were in one of the staterooms which was packed with wooden double tier bunks and, as we drifted in, it was every man for himself in grabbing a bunk. After that came the sorting out as swaps were made in order to be near friends. Once settled in, a meal was laid on as we lined up once more in a queue for the dining room, this not being quite so elegant as in peacetime, since, with the numbers on board, space was at a premium with tables packed tightly across the room. We ate and then retired for the night.

When we woke the next morning, Armistice Day 1941, we were already under way. It was a very grey archetypal November sky and atmosphere that pervaded the Firth of Clyde as we slowly made our way out of the estuary to sea to join the convoy. This exercise was to take another day or so which enabled us to take stock. Apart from about 400 U/T aircrew the ship was packed with army reinforcements for the Eighth Army together with a BBC unit and a Crown Film team. Every space on the liner was occupied, most of the troops using hammocks in the holds. Each unit was allotted a daily timetable for meals to which strict adherence was necessary to ensure smooth running of the ship. Being late put one back in the queue which gave a feeling of guilt as though an interloper trying to obtain an extra meal.

By the second day, as we left the sight of land, the convoy had taken shape being mainly passenger liners, including the *Capetown Castle*, the newest addition to the Union Castle Line's fleet in a position ahead of our *Arundel Castle*, with the *Monarch of Bermuda* to starboard, probably about thirty ships in total, with six warships as escorts.

At this stage no official indication of our destination had been given nor the probable length of our journey, so we just settled down to a routine of exercise and lectures until, after a few days, one of those strange decisions was made which was almost the hallmark of the services. In spite of the fact that on board were nearly 2,000 troops trained in weaponry, volunteers were selected from the RAF embryo aircrew for air defence against possible attacks as we were heading south towards the Bay of Biscay. Although we had no actual gunnery experience, presumably the powers-that-be decided that we were more likely to recognize enemy aircraft rather than start firing on some hapless RAF Coastal Command plane. The twenty of us selected were grateful for the relief from boredom which the job offered as, after a brief course in the use of a Bren gun, we took up various positions on the ship in pairs for our duties on a rota basis, four hours on, four hours rest. After the first night in the cold winter conditions with only service uniforms and greatcoats to keep us warm, some of the crew noted our plight and we then had an issue of sweaters and duffle coats to keep us a little warmer. Somewhere in the Imperial War Museum archives are probably some film and sound recordings made by the BBC war correspondents and the Crown Film Unit in those last two months of 1941 depicting life on board a troopship. We certainly went through our paces to look intent and intelligent as we scoured the skies, more for their cameras than for German aircraft, and laid on the deck stripping down and reassembling a Bren gun in the shortest possible time.

We continued steaming in a general southerly direction and found it quite exhilarating standing high on the decks feeling the ship rising and falling away and watching the other big liners going up and down in the forty foot waves off the Bay of Biscay. During this period the queues shortened considerably on the mess deck as sea sickness afflicted many of the troops and not a few of my friends in the ranks of the U/T aircrew. Our proximity to Gibraltar was signalled by a complete change of escorts and the waves began to abate as we continued south with the temperatures beginning to rise. Soon we were able to stand down from our anti-aircraft duties and orders were given to change over to tropical dress. Word began to circulate that we were about to call in at Freetown and hopes were high for the chance of gaining shore for a short period. All that disappeared from our minds as for the last forty-eight hours before we reached our port of call the nights were rendered almost sleepless due to the sound of intermittent depth-charges being fired by our escorts. Apparently, it was not unusual for U-boats to lay in wait for shipping off Sierra Leone but, fortunately, due to the navy's vigilance, they only succeeded in depriving us of a couple of nights' sleep as we lay in our bunks on the qui vive just in case we had to swim for it. Relief came as the ships sailed in to anchorage in Freetown and the boom closed across the harbour.

Now came the worst part of the voyage. For nearly a week the convoy anchored at the mouth of the river off Freetown while supplies, fuel and water were renewed. No one was allowed ashore and we just sweltered in the humid heat. It would probably have been worse on shore, for, even on board, it was almost compulsory when on deck to smear anti-mosquito cream on exposed parts. Some amusing relief came from the bum-boat boys as they traded fresh fruit with us or gave an exhibition of their swimming and diving skills to retrieve what we threw to them in exchange. But, apart from that, a very large number of us passed the time of day queuing up for treatment of prickly heat by the MOs. It was with great relief that, after a week, we eventually steamed out of the estuary and into the fresh cool air of the open sea. A general routine of roll-call, drill, exercise and study continued each morning with the afternoon left free which, in my case, was devoted to sitting on a deck playing solo whist, the profits from which enabled me to pay for all my cigarettes and drinks for the rest of the voyage, leaving my pay intact. A short while out of Freetown the announcement of the attack on Pearl Harbor was made over the ship's tannoy and our escort became strengthened by the addition of the battleship *Queen Elizabeth* against the possibility of attack by the Japanese as we were heading round the Cape to the Indian Ocean.

News began to circulate that our destination was Durban and our morale was lifted with stories from the crew of the sort of welcome and hospitality we were likely to receive there. We docked during the night, six days before Christmas, and within a short time we were disembarked and ensconced eight to a bell tent in a transit camp, Clairwood, a short distance from Durban. Fortunately, although living in tents, our food was served in more permanent wooden mess huts but, even so, sand seemed to permeate nearly everything we ate and drank, although after wartime diet in Britain the abundant supplies of meat, fruit, jam and other items more than made up for the inconvenience.

In this transit camp we had no duties other than keeping our tents and kit in good condition and being available for roll-call each morning with possible movement orders which usually arrived before midday. As soon as lunch was over we all vacated the camp and took ourselves off by train to Durban. We had, of course, arrived at the hottest time of the year and the thought in those days of spending Christmas in such heat was a novel experience. By the 23rd December nearly everyone had invitations to Christmas dinner somewhere or other but Dick Tucker, Ken Howson, Frank Whittaker and I still wandered round the town wondering where the well-known hospitality of Durban was to be found. Suddenly, it all happened. Crossing the square in the centre of the town, we were, literally, hi-jacked in the middle of the road and propelled into an adjacent hall full of British servicemen being entertained with food and drink. Our captor, Mrs Kay Allen, seemed much relieved when, after questioning, we admitted to being free on Christmas Day and, even more so, when we were pleased to accept her invitation to join her for the day.

For the remainder of our stay in Durban we were entertained by Kay and George, her husband, visiting friends and the races, swimming on the beach, watching the Zulus dancing on Sundays and generally divorcing ourselves from the life we had just left in Britain. It seemed strange seeing-in the New Year in shirts and shorts with a sun blazing down, but we were young and nothing if not adaptable taking such things in our stride. A week into the New Year and it was time to say goodbye to Durban as our posting came through. Ken and I had become quite attached to Kay and, indeed, she to us in a motherly way: so with promises to keep in touch we left by train for our new base.

None of us had any experience of the vastness of South Africa until we made this first long train journey lasting three days. There was no direct line between Durban and Port Elizabeth so we had to go into the interior and then back again. Names of small towns brought to mind that other war fought some forty years previously across this land. Eventually we arrived at the South African Air Force station just outside Port Elizabeth, where we became No.7 Air Observers Course at 42 Air School and it was here that we were to learn our trade to prepare us for war.

Chapter II

First Flight and Crewing Up

We were lucky to be posted to Port Elizabeth, a predominantly English-speaking South African town since it was first colonized in the early nineteenth century. Many of our former friends from ITW and shipboard days were posted to stations up-country in Afrikaner areas where life was not so pleasant out of camp. Whereas we enjoyed a rather warm English summer type climate and were free to wander at will in our spare time, they were subject to a very hot dry climate and were wise only to leave camp in threes as a protection against possible attack by the odd bunch of Afrikaner thugs attached to the Nazi ideals who, fortunately, were a minority.

Our accommodation was dormitory style based in long huts with a door at each end and ten beds on either side. Thus the majority of the twenty-eight cadets on Course 7 were together in one hut and so tended to become a close-knit community. Although a South African airfield, all of the ground instructors were RAF personnel with civilian ex-merchant navy officers looking after the navigational instruction. A number of staff pilots were South African Air Force and several RAF NCO gunnery instructors had seen service in Malta and the Middle East and were now resting, which did bring us a little closer to the realities of war.

For the first week we began our initiation into the art of air navigation and, in particular, map-reading with familiarisation of the surrounding terrain as disclosed on the maps. The course was divided into three parts, navigation, bombing, and gunnery, the first being the longest and most difficult, and requiring a 'pass' before proceeding to the other two. And so we began to learn of navigation theory and plotting, astro-navigation, compasses, meteorology, maps and charts, instruments, directional finding wireless telegraphy, photography, ship recognition, aircraft recognition and virtually everything else that was needed to get an aircraft from A to B, except for the actual flying.

Came the day, 19th January 1942, for our first flying experience, before which it was necessary to learn how to correctly adjust and wear a parachute harness. The ones we used were observer type and stayed the same throughout the war, being used by most aircrew on heavy bomber aircraft, although some pilots did switch to the seat type in the later stages of the war. They consisted of a harness with two straps pulled over the shoulders and straps coming from the back which were pulled through the legs terminating with a quick-release mechanism into which the shoulder straps were clipped. When training we always drew a harness from stores for each flight and consequently always had to adjust the straps for tightness for our particular size, which was a bit of a bore, but essential in case of use.

The standard aircraft throughout the war for navigational training was the Avro Anson, a very reliable twin-engined monoplane. It was just as well that the Cheetah engines always kept going since, until later marks, the Anson did not fly well on one engine and loss of such power usually signalled the necessity for a landing as soon as possible. It was during the first week that we also received one of the few lessons on baling out and landing by the use of parachute. This exercise mainly consisted in practicing how to collapse on to the left shoulder at the point of one's feet touching the ground, usually after jumping from a stand a few feet off the ground. Our first day's flying was made up of one and a half hours in the morning followed by a two hour trip after lunch and during these flights we were intro-duced to the big bore of Anson flying, winding up and down the undercarriage by hand, some 120 turns, if I remember rightly. This was a job always delegated by the pilots to us trainees and, because the handle was positioned to be wound by the pilot, anyone else was not in the best position to do the job, so it was always an awkward task from a somewhat cramped situation.

Air-sickness was a problem for some of the cadets and persisted almost every trip for one or two as it was summer and invariably there was a build up of cumulus cloud very soon after sunrise which normally produced bumpy conditions, particularly over the mountains. As with being at sea, it was a matter of riding with the movement and I never experienced the slightest pang. Rather like Nelson, there were the odd one or two trainees who never seemed to conquer sickness and I remember that Bill Marsh, a former London bus driver, was still suffering from this almost to the end of the course.

Although the war was going badly at this time we seemed to be screened from all that nastiness, and routine continued on the basis of a five and a half day week. The weather at Port Elizabeth was very pleasant and, although it was sometimes very hot, being on the coast, the heat was often modified by a breeze blowing in from the sea but, anyway, as the course progressed, we were moving out of summer into autumn. In the evenings we were free to go into town to the cinema or for a drink and the weekends were often spent on the beaches around Port Elizabeth. Many of us were befriended by the inhabitants, the majority of whom were of British stock. Dick Tucker and I spent quite a time with the McGregors whose daughter introduced us to other friends of our own age with whom we had many enjoyable excursions.

With the advance of the Japanese in South East Asia a vague sense of danger began to manifest itself on the coastal areas of South Africa and some of our navigation exercises were turned into searches over the Indian Ocean. After the freedom we had enjoyed on Saturdays and Sundays we did not particularly take to the idea of one or two weekends being used to carry out evacuation exercises from the base, more so, as this included being issued with .303 rifles (we weren't trusted with ammunition), and sleeping out in the dunes overnight. However, it did bring some sense of reality to balance the almost idyllic existence we were enjoying so far from the centres of battle. This was also reinforced by instructors in the shape of NCO aircrew who were periodically posted in to the air school from Malta and the Middle East after completing their tours, which, while bringing us into contact with war, did not inspire any of us towards getting a posting in that theatre. It was quite obvious to even our inexperienced ears that flying in the Middle East would mean having to use inferior and obsolete machines and equipment rather than what we saw as the exciting new four-engined aircraft with which, we gathered, Bomber Command was now operating.

At this stage of the war we were still being trained as air observers, with the flying 'O' as our badge at the end of the course. This meant that we were expected to be able to do everything in the aircraft except piloting; that is, navigation, bombing, photography, wireless operation and gunnery. Navigation was, of course, based on dead reckoning (DR) with the use of visual pinpoints, visual compass bearings, wireless bearings and astro-navigation. With fairly good weather it was very difficult to get lost in South Africa since any river, town, road or railway was readily recognized because of the scarcity of such features. Even with night-flying (of which we did very little, only seven and a half hours) it was difficult to lose the lights of Port Elizabeth, from which we did not go too far, as the main purpose of night-flying was to obtain practice in the use of the sextant and develop confidence in astro-navigation.

The whole course was school all over again and, since most of us had barely left it, we continued to act rather like schoolboys. At the end of the navigation course and in spite of high marks in most subjects, I got lumbered with the, probably deserved, "could have done better had he worked harder" type of assessment.

Having done the hard slog of navigation for twelve weeks, at the beginning of April we moved across to the fun part of the course, bombing and gunnery. After a week or so learning about the make-up and uses of various bombs and all about terminal velocity and the Mark IX bombsight we then made acquaintance with the Battle, the single-engine light bomber, squadrons of which had been decimated by the Luftwaffe during the Battle of France. While the cockpit might have been comfortable for the pilot the rest of the aircraft was not endowed with comforts for the other aircrew. Entry was by means of the open cockpit halfway along the fuselage which opened into a rather bare compartment between that and the bulkhead behind the pilot, communication with whom was carried on by the use of a speaking tube. The maintenance and reliability of the aircraft was always up for discussion and, although we were young and game for anything, there were plenty of hair-raising stories of dicing in Fairey Battles. I remember one day having to take off three times in three different aircraft, the first two proving unserviceable once we were in the air. For all that, I have no recollection of any of the aircraft actually crashing. So we went through our bombing and gunnery courses and having dropped some fifty-five practice bombs and fired some 1,700 rounds from a Vickers machine gun, we were considered by the 16th May to be adequately prepared for further training back home. We were presented with our flying 'O' brevet by Air Commodore de Broke and immediately found ourselves promoted to sergeants and packing up ready to entrain for Cape Town.

Three days on the train and we arrived at Pollsmoor, the transit camp just outside Cape Town, which seemed to indicate that we were bound for home rather than the Middle East. Stuart Sloan, Bob Frost and Jim Clark had been given the address of a friend, Miss Philip, to contact once we arrived and I was fortunate to be invited to join them when we met up. For the next two weeks, while we awaited our posting, we were driven all around to see the sights abounding in the area, to the Groote Constantia in the wine growing region, the Rhodes Memorial in its most impressive setting high up overlooking the surrounding countryside and many beautiful drives around the glorious coast. Concerts and film shows filled in the remaining hours as, once the morning orders had come or not come through, we were free for the rest of the day.

Inevitably this idyllic period came to an end and on 3rd June it was time to be entrained to the docks where we embarked on a 20,000 ton Orient Line ship, the name of which went unrecorded. This time there was no convoy to assemble as we were to proceed home at speed in company with the *Duchess of Atholl* and escorted by four destroyers or frigates. There were only 200 aircrew on our ship with the only other passengers being a large group of Vichy French army personnel who had been captured by the Free French in the recent Madagascar campaign. There was little organized activity for us on the voyage so, two or three days out, it came as somewhat of a diversion when a plot was discovered whereby the Vichy French were planning to seize the ship and sail her to a French port. So now, instead of manning machine guns against German air attack, as on the way out, I was manning a Lewis gun pointing down on the decks every time the prisoners were allowed up for exercise. The situation was defused somewhat when a destroyer came alongside to remove the ringleaders but the threat remained until we sailed into Freetown and disembarked our potential enemies. A week later we sailed into the Clyde and were sent on a long leave of three weeks before being required to report to Bournemouth. Here we were assembled and told that, due to the need for a new specialist category on heavy bombers, we had now all been remustered to become bomb aimers. I remember that in true services tradition we were advised that we had all volunteered! Our stay in Bournemouth lasted for a week or so during which time I became acquainted with the delights of attending a concert or two by the Bournemouth Symphony Orchestra before we were dispersed to various AFUs (advanced flying units).

Number 9 AFU was at a pre-war RAF station at Penrhos near Pwllheli in north-west Wales and, it being quite a small station, some of us were billeted out in the nearby village of Llanbedrog which was at the head of a beautiful secluded bay, ideal for swimming in the evenings of late July and early August. For much of the flying, on Ansons again, we were sent to Llandwrog, a satellite of Penrhos, near Caernarvon. The airfield had only just been completed and the facilities left a lot to be desired but it did give the opportunity to explore another part of the world new to us since joining the air force. All our efforts were directed towards accurate map-reading and bombing exercises, with some photography thrown in, since that was where our future duties would lie as bomb aimers. Time sped by and because of the pressure to increase the strength of Bomber Command the gunnery section of the course was cut short, with just one short trip on a Blenheim, before we were posted to 15 OTU (operational training unit) at RAF Harwell.

Arriving at Harwell at the end of August we were still segregated in 'trades' with our training intensified to bring us up-to-date on current practice, bombing equipment and weapons in Bomber Command, but the flying we carried out in the second two weeks of September on Ansons was done in conjunction with navigators. In this way we began to assess the capabilities of likely future crew mates since we knew that it would be at this unit that we would have to decide with whom we were going to fly in the future.

All aircrew were volunteers and, wisely, the powers-that-be generally allowed aircrew to decide with whom they wished to fly. And so, for the first two weeks or so at OTU, we were all on the look-out for kindred spirits when we chatted to instructors or mixed with other aircrew in the mess. When we reported to OTU a group of pilots was also posted in who were undergoing conversion to Welling-tons and at the same time were probing around looking for likely crew members. Came the end of September and, one morning, without any preamble or warning we were all taken to a large hall, pilots, bomb aimers, navigators, wireless operators and rear gunners, where the senior instructor announced that we were to crew up and then promptly left us to sort ourselves out. I have never discovered who the genius was who devised the system but, on the whole, it worked brilliantly as the pilots, who had done their homework with the instructors, worked their way through the groups looking for some of the names they had heard of and chatted with others to see if they had an affinity. Most of the navigators and bomb aimers knew each other from flying together over the last month and so there was a certain amount of horse-trading as individuals swapped around to get into a group with whom they saw themselves compatible. Having turned down a pilot who had already selected a navigator in whom I did not have much faith I came together with Dave Hewlett, an above-average pilot, and navigator Harry Blackallar. After a little further chasing around we added 'Chiefie' Beale, wireless operator, who had completed a tour on Hampdens in 1941, and Andy Reilly, from Dublin, as our rear gunner. We were now a full Wellington crew.

Late in September we moved to Hampstead Norris, a newly-built satellite airfield of Harwell and for the next week or so we spent some time in getting to know each other while familiarising ourselves with the Wellington; carrying out dinghy and 'baling out' drill with the odd visit to the local swimming baths for practical use of a dinghy. Dave Hewlett, the son of a publican in the village of Woodmansterne, Surrey, had trained in America and under his leadership we quickly gelled together, spending much time in the local pubs. Andy Reilly, the rear gunner, was a bubbly Irishman whose voice used to go up a pitch when he was excited. He and Dave, both with an interest in the horses, hit it off from the word go and any race meeting in the vicinity of where we were based was a sure attraction. Harry Blackallar (Blackie), the navigator, was the product of a minor public school and was a bit of an enigma, very likeable and effervescent, but subject to petty, almost depressive and childish moods from time to time. He came from Littlehampton but no mention was ever made of his family. He was a good navigator, providing everything was going right, but had a tendency to get into a panic if he slipped up along the line with any calculations. As we progressed together I learnt to give him the necessary support when it was needed and we became a close-knit navigational team. Finally, our wireless was in the hands of Norman Beale. He was a flight sergeant, as against the rest of us being mere sergeants, so he automatically became 'Chiefie'. He was the tallest in the crew and very slim, quiet, but exceedingly reliable. During his first tour the Hampdens had a very tough time, not really having been designed for long night trips and many of his operations had been against Hamburg from which they had received a mauling. With the long homeward leg over the North Sea there were times when Norman had to chuck equipment overboard in order to lighten the weight and so stay in the air.

As usual, switching from a peacetime airfield to one of the wartime variety was not normally a morale-boosting exercise as we were now housed in Nissen Huts, but this change was forgotten as we faced the chance to get to grips with a 'real' aircraft at last. With the introduction of the role of bomb aimer in mid-1942, second pilots had been dropped from the normal manning of bombers and the bomb aimer designated as second pilot in the event of injury to the skipper. Consequently, since arriving at Harwell, I, with other bomb aimers, had been introduced to the Link Trainer for practice in handling controls and instrument flying and this training was intensified at Hampstead Norris.

The five members of our crew now began to get together more and more as we started to fly, train, eat, sleep and drink together almost as one. For the latter half of October we carried out daylight flights only, doing cross-country trips and timing ourselves to arrive at a bombing range to drop up to a dozen 20lb practice bombs, sometimes carrying out air to sea firing in the Irish Sea. As we did not carry a front gunner, I was able to improve my knowledge of turrets and Browning machine guns. By the end of the first week of November we were considered capable of operating at night and we then repeated the flying programme in the dark but invariably having Northampton power station as our target which we had to photograph using an infrared film camera.

At this time, all the aircrew being trained at No.15 OTU Harwell were designated for posting to the Middle East and, as the time was approaching for the completion of our operational training, we were all lined up for a whole batch of inoculations, including yellow fever, which put quite a number of trainees out of action for a day. Within two days of undergoing this experience, Bomber Command, at last, had its way and all postings to the Middle East ceased with immediate effect. On 23rd November 1942 we carried out a last training exercise from Hampstead Norris in daylight incorporating some air to sea firing and the dropping of live 250lb high explosive bombs. Seven days leave followed and, on return, we found ourselves posted with several other crews, including three piloted by New Zealanders, to 102 Squadron Conversion Flight at Pocklington in Yorkshire.

*   *   *

We arrived by train on 4th December, late afternoon, in the dark at Pocklington railway station and, after a short wait, clambered aboard a truck sent to ferry us to the airfield. As it was late we were taken to our quarters in a Nissen hut and settled in before proceeding to the sergeants' mess for a meal and a jar. Here we began to learn the reality of what we had got into as we found that the squadron had lost three aircraft the night before including a flight commander who was carrying the newly-appointed wing commander of nearby 77 Squadron as second pilot for operational experience. In the next week we were to see this figure doubled which brought home to us the high risk nature of the business on which we were due to embark. There was also a shadow hanging over the squadron due to the loss of a well-liked commanding officer, Wing Commander Bintley, who had been hit and killed by another aircraft while landing away at Holme on Spalding due to fog at Pocklington towards the end of October. Sadly, the wingco had recently become highly proficient at landing on the SBA (standard beam approach) recently installed, and had he ordered air traffic control to switch it on, he would probably have been able to land quite safely at Pocklington.

The next morning held much excitement as we walked to the mess and all around us, standing at various distances at dispersals off the perimeter track of the airfield, were large four-engined aircraft, black underneath with brown and green camouflage on the top surfaces. These were the Halifaxes that we would come to know and love (as well as throwing curses in their direction when they failed to come up to scratch). We also discovered that, while our posting was to 102 Squadron Conversion Flight, the unit had undergone a change of name and was now 1652 Conversion Flight.

December dragged a little, with no flying for the crew, as Dave Hewlett was engaged in learning about the aircraft and undergoing conversion to flying on four engines after only being competent with two. For the rest of us, for much of the time, we were involved with our own specialist sections on the conversion flight to learn about the new equipment with which we had to deal. During this time, as bomb aimer, I got to know Eric Hargreaves, the bombing leader, who had completed a tour with 102 Squadron, as we were introduced to the Mark XIV bombsight, bomb distributor panel and GEE. Later, I was to serve under him as an instructor at RAF Rufforth. There was also the need to keep up with practice on the Link Trainer and learn the cockpit and fuel tank layout and switching in order to act as second pilot as well as practicing, always practicing, our sextant shots, the accuracy of which were to prove vital on long trips in the coming months. We also had to acquire two new members of crew, a flight engineer, and a mid-upper gunner, needed to make up a seven-man crew. In December and January we all practiced dinghy drill including the use of a dinghy in the swimming baths at York. In this period we, as a trainee crew, were diverted for a day, with others, to bury seven crew members of a squadron Halifax which had collided on circuit in the early hours of the morning with a 77 Squadron Halifax from nearby Elvington. The burial took place at the parish churchyard of Barmby Moor at the end of the main runway. This sort of collision was an operational hazard waiting for any tired aircrew as they circled their airfield preparatory to landing. The circuit of nearly every airfield in Bomber Command overlapped with that of at least one and most often two other airfields, as in the case of Pocklington. As the norm was to circle anti-clockwise this meant that the aircraft on the other circuits were all flying towards your own so the closing speed was in the nature of 300mph and not many Bomber Command airfields got through the war without at least one collision. Again, we learnt a salutary lesson that bodies did not come out whole from crashed aircraft, for it was obvious from the weights that we were not bearing complete bodies and, as a crew, we learnt the lesson, so that, throughout our coming tour, we never let up our vigilance until we had landed and cleared the aircraft.

The Nissen huts we occupied housed a dozen or so and had recently been constructed to house the additional aircrews going through the conversion flight. My bed was at the end of the hut to one side of the door not in use. One morning I awoke to find the foot of the bed covered in snow blown in through the ventilator over the door which had been installed upside down. Later that day we were all supplied with brooms and shovels to sweep the main runway free of the white stuff. As the measurements of this piece of concrete was fifty yards wide and a mile long it was quite a job even for the 200 or so of us employed on the task. Fortunately, by lunchtime the squadron was stood down for the night and we were all released from our task.

Christmas came and the usual RAF station frolics took place with a football match between the NCOs and the officers for a barrel of beer before we all joined together to serve Christmas dinner to other ranks. Apart from these diversions we welded together as a crew, nearly always going off the base as a group to drink at The Buck and The Feathers in Pocklington High Street or journey by bus to York for various activities. It was often necessary in wartime to move from pub to pub as drinks were in short supply and often pubs ran out halfway through the evening. The beer at this stage of the war had become almost just coloured water with little strength and Andy eventually persuaded me to start drinking Guinness which was a little more effectual but I never really took to the taste so would follow it up with a whisky. This actually became a catch twenty-two situation as the whisky was becoming a little raw and fiery due to the mature stuff being exported for dollars. Consequently, the spirit removed the taste of Guinness but this had to be immediately supped again to prevent my throat being burnt out.

As January 1943 opened all the crew began to get worried as Dave had to fly on ops as a 'second dickie' (second pilot), with an experienced crew to gain knowledge of operations before commencing on his own. This usually covered two or three ops with different pilots but, however experienced the crew, no one could give a guarantee that they would come back complete with our pilot and, therefore, the situation was a bit fraught. If we lost Dave, we would all probably have to return to OTU to find ourselves another pilot.

We had come to Pocklington as a five-man crew but the Halifax had a manning requirement of seven and the conversion unit was the place where the other two joined in. The most important need was for a flight engineer and these were mostly recruited from ground staff from units all over the country and who, until joining the conversion flight, had little flying experience, so that, during the pilots' conversion flying the trainee engineers would also be under instruction. Dave had selected a Geordie, Eric (Joe) Holliday, who we immediately welcomed into the fold. An extra air gunner was also needed and, as it was necessary for the two gunners to have an understanding, Dave took Andy's advice and settled on Willie Hall, who hailed from Belfast. As a consequence, we always had two sides of the Irish question represented to engage us in argument when we were free from German interference. In the last week in January, Dave had convinced the instructors that he was capable of flying Halifaxes on his own and we flew again as a crew. A few days later we had flown about fifteen hours together in daylight on Halifaxes, sufficient to know where everything was, and on 5th February 1943 we were posted to 102 Squadron, where we were allocated to B Flight. We bid farewell to a number of friends who had trained with us and who were now posted to other squadrons, mainly 10 and 77, based on satellite airfields of Pocklington. After eighteen months of training and since we joined up at ACRC in London in July 1941, Frank Whittaker and I were still together at the end of any alphabetical queue but sadly, after two or three months on operations with 102, he, with his New Zealand skipper and crew were posted to Pathfinders and, within a short time, were reported as 'missing'. By the end of that summer, of the twenty-eight trainee observers on No.7 Course at Port Elizabeth, to the best of my knowledge, only seven of us would still be flying.

With our new status at Pocklington, now members of the squadron, we were transferred to new quarters in wooden huts near to the sergeants' mess. The huts were divided into small individual rooms and, although they did not have any washing facilities which were housed in a separate hut, it was the first time since joining the air force that I had private quarters.

We had had no experience of night-flying in a Halifax and so we were immediately detailed on a couple of four/five hour cross-country flights, in-between which Dave did a third second dickie trip while the rest of us prayed that he would return safely. Our prayers were answered and we were now ready to operate.

Chapter III

The Real Thing

It is difficult to attempt to portray to the inexperienced the reality of the conditions or atmosphere on an operation in a heavy bomber. There have been many attempts made to reproduce actions on film and TV but, somehow, most of them have verged either on parodies or, at the other extreme, rather like models for how operations should be conducted, with clipped strict intercom procedural language culminating in direct hits on clearly identifiable targets. But it was very rarely like that. There was no standard, every trip throwing up something different from those previously carried out with the three variable enemies; aircraft reliability, the Germans and the weather all playing their part in different ways and proportions: the Germans often being the least of our worries. In most films it appears as though night-bombing was conducted in formations with other aircraft being visible but such shots were almost always the subject of dramatic licence. In real life, once airborne, each crew was on their own, hidden in the dark and conscious only of other unseen aircraft by the occasional bump of the plane when hitting the slipstream of another 'heavy', or panic stations as a large black shape would suddenly appear cutting in from above or below with the pilot having to take violent evasive action to avoid collision. Sometimes another heavy would come close to fly alongside for a short period but one soon broke away, for two aircraft together made a better target for the enemy.

The only common factor on all raids was the crew, the same other six members on whom you relied and with whom there was a strong bond of dependency. Each relied on the others to do their job and, aware of the strengths and idiosyncrasies of the other crew members, knew when a word of support or other help was needed, such knowledge gained from flying together for several months. All recognised that life or death could be the outcome of any flight depending on how well the team worked together.

On a bomber station it was usual, after breakfast, for aircrew to report to their respective sections, pilots to the flight offices, bomb aimers to the bombing section, navigators to navigation section and so on. Here the flight commander or section leader would bring everyone up-to-date on the latest information on equipment or orders whilst waiting for the day's order of battle to appear, which was the indication that operations were 'On', or 'Off' as the case may be.

On 13th February 1943 we were detailed for our first raid as a crew. For Chiefie Beale it was back in the old routine and, of course, Dave Hewlett had done three trips as second dickie so he also knew the drill. The rest of us in the crew now knew what "butterflies in the tummy" meant as we went about our tasks during the morning, making all the necessary checks on our equipment in the aircraft. Later, I watched as the armourers loaded the bombs and SBCs onto the aircraft. There were fifteen bomb positions in a Halifax, nine in the main bomb bay in the fuselage and three in each wing. For this trip we were to carry four 1,000lb HE, two small bomb containers (SBCs) of eight 30lb incendiaries in each and nine SBCs each of ninety-six 4lb incendiaries; an overall bomb load of four tons. While this was going on, Chiefie was checking his wireless and Andy his guns. Although Willie was the mid-upper gunner, at this period the Halifax IIs were not carrying any front or mid-upper turrets, both had been removed as the original large and bulbous turrets produced too much drag which reduced speed by as much as seven knots. The nose had been faired over pending re-design and it was intended to replace the mid-uppers by a smaller and lower profile turret but there was insufficient production in the autumn of 1942 to carry out the change. As a consequence we had a small Perspex cupola in the floor of the aircraft near the rear escape hatch to enable the mid-upper gunner to cover the blind spot under the aircraft and thus prevent any under tail attacks. Perhaps, in the light of later experience of schräge musik (upward-firing cannon), we would have lost less aircraft by retaining the cupola instead of replacing the turret.

In the late afternoon the detailed crews, eleven in all, assembled in the briefing room with the section leaders, navigation, bombing, wireless, gunnery and flight engineering sitting in the front, and individual crews sitting together. As soon as everyone had assembled, we all stood as in strode the wingco, George Holden, accompanied by the station commander, Group Captain Young, soon to be superseded by North-Carter, which was certainly a change for the better. The door of the briefing room was shut with a guard posted outside and briefing commenced. Up to this point only the pilots and navigators were aware of the target location, since briefing was left as late as possible for security reasons but navigators had to prepare their charts and flight plans.

Over the last year a big change had been brought about in Bomber Command operations leaving less initiative to individual squadrons and crews with regard to timing and routes. These were planned by Command in conjunction with the Group AOCs as soon as targets were set and all aircraft had to conform. The principle of the bomber stream had been developed so that all the aircraft were concentrated in a continuous belt, all flying at predetermined heights and speeds to arrive at given times at the various points on route, the idea being that the German radar would not be able to pick out individual aircraft on which to direct AA fire or nightfighters. Get out of that stream, either by going high or low, or being off course and you immediately became a predicted target for the enemy guns or fighters.

Once the CO had taken his seat, the nod was given to the intelligence officer who now drew the curtain covering the whole of the end wall to reveal the map of Western Europe on which a tape had been pinned showing the route from base to and from the target.

Tonight it was to be Lorient and we heaved a sigh of relief that our first trip was to be on a comparatively easy target. Although classified as 'easy', there were still the fighter defences and various flak batteries to cope with. Since the fall of France the Germans had been using the western ports of France from which to operate their U-boats, about which the admiralty were very concerned. The enemy, anticipating bombing, had by now constructed massive reinforced concrete shelters under which the U-boats were protected and against which none of the bombs we carried at that time were able to penetrate. The only strategy was to raze the dock area to make it as difficult as possible for the Germans to service the port, although no mention was made of this at the time.

The intelligence officer, Squadron Leader Hart, ran through the reasons for attacking Lorient, strength of raid (466 aircraft), the effect of U-boats in the Atlantic and the necessity for denying the facility to the enemy. Usually this was followed by the met officer giving the weather forecast in terms of conditions on route and over target and, of great interest, landing conditions on return with possibilities of diversionary airfields in event of bad weather. In turns the various section leaders stood up to stress the different essential duties of the crew members. The navigation leader highlighted any navigational difficulties and possible landmarks, avoiding heavily defended areas as at this stage the PFF were not yet laying down route markers. The bombing leader explained the system of marking the target and confirmed the colour of target indicators and priority for bombing, while the flight engineer leader stressed the need for engineers to continually monitor petrol consumption and to check bomb inspection hatches after leaving the target to ensure that all HE bombs had been released, and so on. Eventually, the CO would round off the proceedings with some selected words, adding any messages received from the AOC in C, wishing everyone good luck to bring things to a conclusion. We then departed to our billets or mess depending on what time was left before supper, which invariably consisted of bacon and egg. Sometimes briefing was after supper so that take-off followed on almost immediately. The last thing before leaving the mess was to fill up one's flask with coffee and collect sandwiches before walking over to the Flights to empty pockets of all documents, don flying gear, and collect parachutes and escape packs, as well as orange juice, caffeine tablets, etc.

Now we were ready to go. After eighteen months training here I was, all keyed up, ready to find out the reality of war. We climbed on to a small truck with a couple of other crews going out to our dispersal and set out in the dark round the perimeter track. As we were 'blind' in the back of the truck we relied on the WAAF driver to establish which aircraft dispersal we had reached and, responding to her cry, the individual crews dropped out of the truck with farewells of "Good luck" being exchanged.

We climbed aboard our aircraft and stowed our parachutes, maps and other paraphernalia before disembarking, when we stood around chatting and smoking the last cigarette while waiting for start-up time to tick up. The 13th February was a Saturday and our aircraft was R-Robert as we were part of B Flight, 102 still being a two flight squadron. Aircraft around the airfield were now beginning to splutter into life and the full-blooded roar of Merlin engines began to fill the night air. It was time for us to go. Led by Dave we embarked and took up positions. For take-off and landing in Halifaxes the navigator and wireless operator sat on the floor in the rest position between the two main spars, with their back braced against the front one, which was a lot safer than sitting in the nose. They were joined by the spare gunner while the rear gunner occupied his turret. This left the pilot at the controls with the bomb aimer sitting alongside to assist with the controls and the flight engineer immediately behind the pilot with a bank of instruments and other items covering the four engines. As time arrived for start-up, Dave called "Contact" through the cockpit window to the member of groundcrew manning the external battery which was used to start the engines to save the aircraft battery system. The port inner engine started to windmill slowly, coughing and spluttering once or twice before suddenly exploding into a roar and was then throttled back to idle while the three other engines, in turn, went through the same procedure. Once the engine-running temperatures were reached, each was run up to speed and the magneto drop tested before being reduced to idle. This was a preliminary must at all times, not just for ops, but to reduce the risk of engine failure on take-off: it all contributed to that tension building up to an operation. A faulty engine usually meant having to abandon the aircraft and changing to the spare located somewhere else on the airfield, which meant a late take-off. Now Dave started to go through the pilot's checks to ensure everything was working properly, before the ground NCO came aboard with the form 700 for him to sign out the aircraft as being in acceptable order. With a "Good luck" or "See you back in the morning", the NCO would then make his way back through the fuselage, close and lock the hatch door through which he had exited, and we were on our own.

In the dark we now slowly moved out of dispersal on to the perimeter track where we joined other aircraft making their way to the end of the runway. We watched as two or three aircraft in front of us turned on to the runway, revved up and trundled along that long stretch of tarmac before rising and vanishing into the dark sky with only the glow of the exhausts showing. Dave ran up the engines again in turn and tested one last time for mag drop before it was our turn and we positioned to line up for take-off. The green Aldis flashed from the control caravan and Dave steadily pushed the four throttles of the Merlin engines forward right through the 'gate' for full boost as I shadowed him with my left hand to prevent any possible spring back, and then reached over to lock the controls. This enabled Dave to use both hands on the stick to control this potentially dangerous stage of the operation. All aircrew who flew in bombers will be aware of the feeling of trepidation as the aircraft began to pick up speed with several tons of high explosive underneath and surrounded by nearly two thousand gallons of high octane spirit. If there was a prayer to be offered at this time it was always, "Please don't let any of the engines cut", for the loss of an engine while the wheels were still on the ground could produce a vicious swing off the runway perhaps ripping off the undercarriage or hitting any object in the way with the consequences which might follow. If the aircraft had just become airborne then there was a danger of just sinking down into the ground, landing straight ahead and hoping there were no houses or trees in the way and that the bombs would not explode and the aircraft not catch fire. None of these things happened to us while we were flying together but they were always in the mind at take-off.

We successfully became airborne at 1837 hours and set course southward down the length of England. Crossing the coast at Start Point we headed across the Channel, I, for one, gazing back at that coast wondering whether it would be the last I ever saw of England. But those thoughts were soon overtaken by the realisation that we were entering the enemy night-fighter zones and would be under risk of attack if we strayed out of the main force stream. As we crossed the French coast I was able to identify our crossing point. On this first trip Blackie and I had not yet reached an understanding that I should operate the GEE set to get the longest range and fed him with positional fixes whenever required giving him the freedom to concentrate on his chart and keep us on course. The Germans were jamming GEE, thus reducing its range so it was essential to use it to its limits in order to get as accurate winds as possible on which to project our navigation. GEE was one of those marvellous pieces of radar devised by our scientists on which we became almost too dependent to the point that some crews often became lost if it went U/S (unserviceable). By it we were able to fix our position almost to within 100 yards over the British Isles and it became invaluable in safely descending through cloud and finding base on return. It had originally had a range reaching out to the Ruhr but since the Germans had started to jam it, the range was reduced to around the Dutch coast and down a little way into France. At this stage of the campaign the strategy was to condense the stream of aircraft so that as many as possible went through the fighter control zones in the shortest time thus making it very difficult for the German controllers to single out individual bombers on which they could vector individual fighters. It was, therefore, essential to maintain position as near as possible to the planned height and track so that we had the protection of a mass of blips on the German radar screens. However, because most of the fighters were further north to protect the German heartland we did not have so much trouble in this corner of north-west France and, provided we stayed on track, we did not expect too many problems with flak.

We were scheduled to arrive on target about three-quarters of the way through the attack and as we progressed we could see the target well and truly lit up with the brilliant coloured target markers outshining the fires raging around them. I checked with Blackie for the latest wind speed and direction and fed this in to the bombsight computer. By now I had taken up the prone position in the nose and began to give advance directions to Dave to steer us to the aiming point. The visibility was good over Lorient so I was able clearly to see the primary AP (aiming point) without any difficulty although the fires raging below almost blotted out the details of the town. I cannot recall what I expected to find on this, my first operation, but I do remember being awed to see the results of the power we were using, of which I was part, and I felt for the French who were below on the receiving end. I then put all such thoughts out of mind and concentrated on the task of guiding Dave in to the aiming point. I called for "Bomb doors open" and then continued to direct him left or right as I located the target marker on the grid in the bombsight. There was a fair share of flak coming up which was a trifle frightening for the first time but it was not concentrated on us and we proceeded to bomb from 10,000 feet without any worries. Upon completion of the bomb run I called for the bomb doors to be closed, remaining on our course until the photoflash had given our camera a photograph of the target area. The photographic system was quite simple. As the bombs were released a photoflash also left the aircraft which was ignited by a barometric fuse at the moment when the bombs hit the ground. At the time the bomb tit was pressed the camera was activated, winding on a new frame with the shutter held open. As the aircraft crossed the target area, traces of various fires on the ground would be recorded and, when the flash lit up the ground, a photo of the town would be taken. Providing the aircraft had kept straight and level from the time of releasing the bombs the centre of the photo would be the point at which the bombs struck.

With a fresh course from Blackie for the trip back we turned away from Lorient and headed for home. As we crossed the south coast we started to descend from our operational height until we reached the Trent Valley. From now on there was no need to worry about high ground and we could safely fly back to base visually at about 2,000 feet but, nevertheless, watching out for other aircraft. This was to become our most-favoured return route back to base since after the tension of the previous hours one, at least, did not have to be concerned about hitting high ground.

After reaching base, we took our place in the circuit and, in due course, landed at 0059 hours after being airborne for over six hours. We parked at dispersal, collected our 'chutes and other paraphernalia from the aircraft and slowly descended out of the aircraft. What a relief to meet the cold night air and fling off our helmets and masks. Those of us who smoked lit up as we waited for the truck to take us back to the crew room lockers and then Intelligence for interrogation. The first thing always was to grab a mug of tea or coffee laced with rum to slake one's thirst before looking around to find an idle intelligence officer. The whole crew settled round the table and the interrogation commenced. This covered a whole series of questions with particular reference to the route we took, adherence to timing, siting of any observed flak positions, fighter activity, weather compared to forecast, any observed losses of bombers with time and position and, of course, the attack itself. The summary of our report on the latter was recorded in the squadron records as follows:

"Attacked primary target at 10,000 feet, good visibility. Identified Scorff River and flew down Eastern bank, and saw bridges. Aiming point identified visually and in bombsight. Large fires in city area and to east of river developing."

We had been in the air for 6hrs 25mins and, of the 466 aircraft scheduled to attack, seven had not returned, but none of these were from 102. And so we drifted off to bed, knowing that we had not been found wanting.

Getting up for lunch the next day we took the day easy, being 'stood down' from ops. But ops were on, as the squadron prepared for an attack on Cologne. Shortly after tea, as the crews made their way out to the dispersals there was some commotion in the mess with everyone dashing to the door from where could be seen a large cloud of black smoke pouring skyward from the other side of the York road. It could only be an aircraft on fire and this was very quickly confirmed as the bomb load and fuel blew up producing a great pyrotechnic display as we all ducked for cover.

The cause of the disaster was the bomb distributor board, known as the Mickey Mouse. This was a device for timing the dropping of the bombs from the fifteen bomb positions in the Halifax, being selected by an arm, operated by clockwork, revolving over electrical contacts. It was standard procedure, prior to take-off, for the bomb aimer to test out the equipment, in particular, checking the run of the clockwork with the switches off. During this two of the SBCs in the wing bomb bay had been released. The 4lb incendiaries had dropped around the wheel, ignited, and within a few seconds flames were leaping from the burning tyre up into the wing. The crew grabbed fire extinguishers and attempted to put the blaze out but the equipment was too puny to deal with the flames, so they gave up and ran off up the York road with the groundcrew in tow. Meanwhile the wingco, George Holden, attracted by the pall of smoke, had driven from the control tower and met the fleeing airmen. Slowing down, he called to them to get back to the aircraft and put the fire out but merely received some choice replies about trying it himself as they continued running in the opposite direction. It was reported afterwards that he reached the burning aircraft, got out to inspect the fire, realized that there was nothing to be done, returned to his car parked under the wing, was unable to start it, and was then seen hareing up the York road in pursuit of the others. A short time later the bombs and aircraft blew up with not much left that was recognizable.

As a corollary to that, Flight Sergeant Hartshorn, a Canadian with 102, was on operations that night and did not return. As Norman Noble, one of his groundcrew, recalls, he and his crew were always together, laughing, joking, leg-pulling and were generally popular all round. Continuing in Norman's own words:

> "This particular night they got off the transport and climbed straight into the aircraft without saying a word to anyone or each other at all. I pulled away the starter battery trolley after the engines had fired, went upstairs with the '700' and waited until the skipper ran up the engines and did all the necessary checks. He throttled back the engines and then just sat there staring into space. I put the 700 in front of him open for the first signature, but he still didn't move. I gave him a pencil, thinking that he probably hadn't one. He signed and gave me the form back. I had to repeat the procedure twice more for the other signatures required. I gave him a pat on the shoulder, 'See you in the morning', and left him still staring. I don't think he heard me. But all the rest of the crew were the same, not a word, not a sound and all sat staring, completely lifeless. It was an atmosphere I have never forgotten. I was the last person to see that crew alive."

Did that crew have a premonition of death? Or was it the effect of the other aircraft being fired and the realization of what they were sitting on? It will never be known. Years later, in the early 70s, Norman Noble and his wife visited York to see the 'Flowers in the Minster' exhibition. It was only the second time he had been to the Minster and after following the queue round the exhibits he was about to exit from the north side when he spotted the RAF Memorial Book recording the 19,000 aircrew who had died whilst flying from Yorkshire bases. Not only was it open at 'H' but at the very page containing the entry 'J.L.Hartshorn, F/Sgt, Pilot 102 Squadron'.

* * *

Three days later on 16th February we were again detailed to attack Lorient, part of a force of 377 bombers of which nine were from 102. We took off at 1843 hours and followed much the same route as on the 13th except that on the return trip, Blackie, our navigator, somehow got a GEE reading wrong and we detoured over Wales before getting back to Yorkshire and landing at 0100 hours. From then on I always operated the GEE set. Our report for the raid read:

> "Attacked primary target at 15,000 feet, Heading 190°T, 215 TAS. Weather at target very good. Identified river with White PFF flares. Aiming point in bombsight. Saw many fires starting in target area."

The 19th February saw us again on the order of battle list, this time being lined up for Wilhelmshaven with ten Halifaxes from the squadron in an attacking force of 195 aircraft. The weather forecast was for a clear target but no guarantee was ever given, as we were to find out. Now for the first time we were going to attack Germany itself, which meant flying through their ground-controlled fighter belt stretching from the north of Denmark, through Holland and Belgium and on towards the west of France. This belt was divided into boxes, each with a night-fighter, controlled from the ground. An individual aircraft flying through the box would be visible on the ground controller's screen which would enable him to vector the fighter on to the intruder. To counter this, Bomber Command had devised the bomber stream so that all aircraft flew on the same track and at given heights, the theory being that it would be impossible to pick out an individual aircraft on the radar screens. However, for various reasons, some bombers were late, some couldn't make the height, some had navigational errors putting them off track, all of which meant that they were showing up as individual blips on the German radar and became potential prey for the hunters.

During my first tour we were never subjected to an attack by night-fighters and I think this was due to good flying by Dave Hewlett and accurate navigation through a good understanding between Blackie and myself with the use of GEE, ground positions and astro-navigation fixes which enabled us to stay in the main stream. Until H2S radar was brought in, most bomber aircraft had an astrograph set above the navigational table which, with the right film and settings for the given star, projected lines of bearing on to the chart. This saved having to calculate physically the bearing and gave a more instant position without the time lapse for calculation.

102 Squadron was part of 4 Group which had pioneered night navigation and bombing in the early years of the war. One of the leading lights of that era was an Australian, Donald Bennett, later to become the AOC of the Pathfinder group, probably the greatest air navigator of that time. One of his disciples had been the navigation officer on the heavy conversion flight at Pocklington, Squadron Leader Lawson, who always pushed the use of astro whenever possible, to the point where we came to rely on it, particularly for long penetrations of the Continent, when there were no other aids. Wing Commander George Holden, our CO, was also an advocate and at every briefing he would stress the importance of the use of astro. On a comparatively short trip like Wilhelmshaven, there was a problem with taking astro shots: it was necessary to fly straight and level for a minimum of two minutes so it was not advisable to carry this out when flying through the fighter belts. An astro shot

required a steady platform for accuracy and for this it was usual to put the aircraft in 'George', the automatic pilot, which could do a better job than any manual control. The bubble sextant in service could be used for single shots but in order to iron out the effects of aircraft movement, was usually used over one to two minutes. A spring-loaded mechanism was wound up and when the first shot was triggered a series of sixty readings were taken which were then averaged out. So the procedure before taking a star shot was to agree with the navigator the best stars to give a good intersection, set up sextant in astro-dome, locate the stars, ask the pilot to put George in, line up sextant on star, press trigger on sextant at the same time as calling to the navigator to record the time and when the shutter came down in sextant to call out again to the navigator.

We had not expected to fly on this night as Blackie had a cold and had been taken off flying but we were allocated a replacement navigator, Sergeant Les Herbert, from another crew. It was not something which we liked but since we had no reasonable objection to Les, or his navigation, having known him at OTU, we accepted the situation. Anyway, he may not have been too keen on flying with us! Little did we or he know that he would be dead six days later.

There must have been an imbalance between A and B Flights of crews and aircraft that night as we had to fly an A Flight aircraft. Our route was fairly straightforward, almost direct across the North Sea after we had taken off at 1819 hours and crossed the Yorkshire coast, climbing to 18,000 feet. The forecast was for cloud over the North Sea, clearing over the target, but it did not quite turn out like that.

Of our ten aircraft, one had to turn back early due to a torn cowling which blew back, causing violent shuddering. It was a fairly quiet trip getting a little lively with AA fire in the target area. A break in the cloud enabled me to see Langeroog and pinpoint Schillig and the coast to the south but thereafter the area was covered in 10/10th cloud. At that time, the Pathfinders (PFF) were still in their infancy and had only ground-marking flares available which were aimed using H2S equipment which had only recently come into use. Even so, Bomber Command instructions were that the main force should always bomb PFF markers. As we came to Wilhelmshaven, the area being completely covered with cloud, we could only aim our load at the red glow generated by the markers below the cloud. For the first trip against Germany itself, the whole thing was a bit of an anti-climax. The return flight was without incident and we landed at 2244 hours.

For the next six nights the squadron did not operate and during that time we were given a forty-eight hour pass. On operational squadrons of Bomber Command it was usual for aircrew to have seven days leave every six weeks, interspersed with forty-eight hour passes. When the squadron was not operating and the CO could think of nothing better for us to do we were normally free after lunch and got off the base for the rest of the day, usually travelling into York or Leeds to attend the cinemas or theatre and ending up in the pubs at night. Among these was Betty's, renowned before the war and since for its cakes and afternoon teas, but during the war known simply as Betty's Bar. We often would rendezvous there for a meal before moving downstairs to the bar known to most airmen as The Dive. This was below street level and during the war had a poor reputation, it being said that one only had to visit there to find out the target for that night, although I can't remember ever receiving confirmation of this for myself.

Our fourth trip, on 25th February was to Nuremburg and after taking off at 1917 hours we headed for Colne Point before crossing the south coast at Dungeness. It was a dark clear night as we flew due east at 15,000 feet with the conditions ideal for astro-navigation and we arrived at the target on ETA. Unfortunately, the PFF were late and the nightmare then took place. We had to circle for fifteen minutes and during that time I think I was more scared than at any other time before or since, but not by the enemy. With the concentration of bombers over the targets there was always the risk of collision, but that was calculated with very long odds as all aircraft were roughly going in the same direction. This was different. There were now some 300 plus aircraft all circling and crossing each others' path and lying in the nose was frightening as black shapes came flitting past from all directions. I had to call out to Dave once or twice since, being in a bank most of the time, he had blind spots to his starboard, and could not pick up bombers closing in on us from that direction. It was fortunate the German night-fighters were not operating efficiently that night otherwise they would have been in their element. Suddenly there was a splash of red to port as a marker was dropped and I hurriedly turned Dave on to the target. There was only about half a minute to line up but something was niggling at me that all was not right. As I pressed the bomb tit the marker was burning out and I realised that it was not quite the right red colour that we used. I had been taken in by a dummy German marker, the first I had come across, and I could not but let loose a few old fashion expletives. After an uneventful return, we landed back at base at 0337 hours after 8hrs 20mins in the air.

In retrospect, I have always been astonished by the interpretation of aircrew reports by the intelligence officers responsible for the interrogation of crews upon return from raids. What we reported was often at variance with the written records and one can only assume that Intelligence recorded what they thought Group and Command would want to hear. Although it was made quite plain that we had attacked a German dummy, our report read:

> "Attacked primary target at 15,000 ft. 189°T TAS 204 knots. Visibility good with considerable ground haze. Target found by DR. PFF not arrived so stood off for 15 mins. till first TI's seen. Ran up to TI which faded just before release. Two fires seen. Conditions good but lateness of PFF made it more difficult than it should have been."

There is sufficient truth for it to be plausible but it skirts round the fact that we knew we had not bombed the target. It would seem to be a leftover from the early days of the war when returning crews, frozen and tired from flying long trips in Whitleys and Wimpies were pressed to make wrong claims. An article written in the early 1950s by a 102 squadron leader flight commander of that time (1940/41) commented:

> "Claims were made in the UK press of having heavily bombed the objective laid down for the night. This was the fault of station intelligence officers who would press crews to say that they had recognized certain points in rivers and other landmarks in the target area and that the target laid down had been bombed. If the crews admitted that they had not recognized the area by any means they were looked at askant and given a black mark. Tired crews soon became alive to this and quickly agreed with the interrogator's deductions and thus got away to bed early. In many cases these exaggerated claims in the press were without foundation."

We had barely woken up the next morning, to learn that one of our aircraft on the way to Nuremburg had crashed over this country with the loss of all the crew. Probably the rudder problem! Then we found ourselves on the order of battle again, this time Cologne. The usual routine preparation was undergone and we took off at 1855 hours heading toward what we then knew to be the deadliest concentration of night-fighters guarding the Third Reich. From thirty miles off the Dutch and Belgian coastlines one could expect to be attacked at anytime all the way to the target and back again on the way out. In addition, there were flak ships constantly moving their position ready to take a bomber by surprise, and the German navy could be deadly accurate with their flak.

Cologne, while not actually in the Ruhr was within the flak belt covering the whole and as we approached we received the usual greeting. The PFF, still somewhat in their infancy, were late again and we had to do three rather large orbits standing off from the target. Even though the night was clear and we could identify the town, there was a certain amount of ground mist and we were under instruction to bomb only on PFF markers. Eventually, they came and I was able clearly to bomb a collection of primary markers just off centre of the city. After an uneventful flight back we landed at 0014 hours. Of the eight aircraft from 102 only six returned. Our report read:

> "Attacked primary target at 15,000 ft. 066 M, IAS 170 kts. No cloud, ground haze. Centre of concentration of green TIs in bombsight. Own results not seen but several sticks seen bursting in target area with many incendiaries starting fires with two large fires in centre of target seen when leaving. Three orbits made before TIs began to fall."

Two nights later, on 28th February, we were again on ops, this time on the submarine base at St. Nazaire. We flew down to the south of England, crossing the coast near Start Point when, shortly afterwards, we had to feather the port inner engine due to a coolant leak. We decided to carry on with three engines and attacked the target, which was clear, although with a great deal of ground haze. Our bombs were seen to fall between the primary and secondary aiming points. Once we left the target we decided to land at our advanced landing base rather than flog up to the north of England on three engines. Exeter was a fighter base and, as such, always welcome for 'landing away'. With many fewer personnel than on a bomber station, there was a lot less pressure on services and bomber crews were always feted when arriving. As we needed to have an engine changed it was a couple of days before we could fly back to Pocklington and we made the most of our stay in Exeter.

Three weeks later, under Group DROs dated 29th March 1943 the following was circulated.

NOTABLE WAR SERVICES

The Air Officer Commanding wishes to bring to the notice of all ranks in the Group, the courage and devotion to duty displayed by No.1295000, Sergeant D.J.Hewlett of No.102 Squadron.

Sergeant Hewlett was the captain of a Halifax detailed to attack St.Nazaire on 28th February 1943. The aircraft had just passed over the enemy coast when the port inner engine failed. The engineer reported overheating due to a coolant leak but the captain, feathering the airscrew, decided to go on to the target although he knew that once he had opened the bomb doors they could not be closed in the normal manner as the hydraulic pumps worked off the unserviceable engine. By skilful flying and determination he kept the aircraft on its course, and maintained height until reaching his objective. When the bomb doors were opened the aircraft lost height and the target was successfully attacked. This done he returned to the advance base he had been instructed to use in an emergency and landed successfully.

We flew back to Pocklington on 2nd March and the following day were detailed to attack Hamburg. During his first tour, Chiefie, our wireless op had had one or two hair raising trips to Hamburg and always held out this city as the ultimate in nastiness. Shortly after crossing the Yorkshire coast our intercom began to give trouble and before long packed up completely, in spite of all that Chiefie could do. We had no choice but to dump our bombs in the North Sea and turn back home. Thereafter, we would always chide Chiefie with having upset the intercom rather than go to Hamburg, a completely false charge, of course.

Two days later, 5th March, we started the campaign that was, at long last, to smash the Ruhr. Oboe had now been tested and was ready to be used against Essen, the heart of the Krupps empire. The Mosquito aircraft using this equipment were controlled by two stations in England which by ranging radar determined the release of the marker flares. No longer would the permanent haze over the Ruhr valley conceal the factories there. This was the first major raid in which Oboe had been used but, since there was only one set of stations in use which could only handle one Mossie at a time, markers could only be dropped every ten minutes. Oboe equipment was rather temperamental and if one Mossie failed to mark there would obviously be another lapse of ten minutes before the next one could be handled. To ensure continuous marking PFF heavies backed up the Oboe markers with a different colour.

We took off at 1941 hours and crossing the Yorkshire coast at Hornsea climbed steadily on track until we reached our operational height of 18,000 feet when we levelled out. Maintenance of track, time, speed and height was important in ensuring protection by the bomber stream from having a fighter vectored on the aircraft as we approached within thirty miles of the enemy coast. Desultory AA fire could be seen to port and starboard as bombers strayed off track and attracted the attention of the coastal defences. We got through without seeing any fighters but as we approached the Ruhr the flak became more and more intense with a continuous thumping of shells bursting in the vicinity. It just did not seem possible to fly through such intense fire and not be hit. The smell of cordite permeated the aircraft as the searchlights latched on to some poor aircraft and caught it, enabling the gunners below to concentrate fire as it struggled to free itself from the lights. Once coned it was often best to turn around, get out, and start another run.

The approach to the target seemed interminable as we slowly crept over the Ruhr to Essen which was already a mass of flames with three really large conflagrations observed. We bombed the target at 18,000 feet and thankfully turned for home although, having come in, we still had to run the gauntlet to get out again. As we turned for home, the hydraulics red warning light came on indicating that either the hydraulics might not be working or we had an electrical fault. We had no means of knowing which. What we did know was that Nick Mattich, a New Zealander friend of ours, had had the same problem over England a few nights previously and nearly fell out of the sky when his bomb doors opened, wheels dropped down and flaps came fully down – all in one go! Dave decided to land as soon as possible after arriving over East Anglia. All the squadrons there seemed to have arrived back well before us and there was not a lighted airfield to be seen. It took four mayday calls to wake anyone. We eventually landed at Swanton Morley at 0010 hours.

The next morning the fault was revealed as purely electrical on the warning light circuit. This was quickly rectified and we were soon on our way back to Pocklington where we landed safely.

Chapter IV

The Big City

Some days passed, kicking our heels, before my crew, having been on the squadron for six weeks, became entitled to Leave and so went our separate ways for the next seven days. A few days after returning we were again on the order of battle for 26th March, this time with Duisburg as the target for the 455 bombers scheduled to attack. Since joining the squadron at the end of January, a matter of seven weeks, we had lost twelve aircraft and, as we rarely had put that number in the air on any one night, it did not require a mathematician to work out that the odds on survival were not good.

As the weather forecast was predicting 10/10th cloud over the target, the briefing was for bombing on sky markers dropped by Oboe Mosquitoes. The markers were flares, usually green or red, suspended on parachutes with barometric pressure detonators set to fire above the cloud height. This was not as accurate as direct marking due to the drift of the flare caused by the wind but, nevertheless, was better than trying to gauge the centre of the glow of markers under the cloud, which could not always be seen, anyway.

We took off at 1957 hours, with a route taking us over the coast at Hornsea from where we set course across the North Sea for Egmond on the Dutch coast, having been allocated Q-Queenie, not a particularly favourite aircraft of anyone on the squadron. It did not climb very well but we managed to get to 18,000 feet some way before reaching Egmond. As predicted, there was 10/10th cloud over north-west Europe with the cloud tops above 5,000 feet. Whether this affected the night-fighter airfields or not is difficult to say but, on the whole, there seemed to be a lack of night-fighter activity approaching and crossing Holland. The Germans had cottoned on to the sky-marking technique and, about twenty miles north of the target, had dropped some flares somewhat similar to ours seeking to divert our bombs from the aiming point. We flew on to our ETA (estimated time of arrival) which coincided with the dropping of a release point flare and bombed on that. The Oboe Mossies had a bad night with several of them suffering malfunction of the equipment, so on the whole the raid was not too successful. We landed at 0028 hours so were in bed by 0230 to get a reasonable night's sleep.

After a late breakfast on 27th March, we found that we were again on the order of battle for the night, one of eight from the squadron, this time it was for the big city – Berlin. We were now truly in the groove and set about the routine of preparation for the trip before attending briefing where we learnt that we were part of a force of 396 heavies attacking the city. By 2000 hours we were airborne on what was to prove a fairly quiet trip as our route brought us in on the south side of the target. It was a clear sky and, using astro-navigation, we stayed on track so that we missed the defensive flak surrounding the Ruhr and other towns on the way, although we saw the odd bomber, which had strayed, getting a pasting as it overflew flak batteries. By staying in the middle of the bomber stream there was no problem with fighters, although there was little evidence of much activity on their part.

Things livened up, however, as we came to Berlin from the south-west with fairly intensive flak coming up left, right and centre, although it seemed more of a barrage than predicted fire. There was no cloud cover and visibility was good with searchlights sweeping everywhere and time, I am sure, stood still as we droned across Berlin. I set the bombsight and started giving Dave directions towards the collection of red and green ground markers around which most of the bombs were being aimed. We were on a heading of 015T at 18,000 feet when I released the bombs towards the centre of the green primary markers with everyone relieved as we turned north-west to get out of the place. After an uneventful flight back home we landed at Pocklington at 0314 hours.

As stated earlier, the main dangers facing aircrew of Bomber Command were the Germans, the weather and, sometimes, inadequate aircraft to do the job. At times the Germans dropped to the bottom of the list and, for us, the next trip was one such night.

Having visited Berlin two nights before it was a bit surprising that on 29th March it was on again, but the word was that Harris wanted another crack at this vital target before the lighter evenings made it too difficult. The weather forecast was appalling and, unofficially, our two met officers at Pocklington were backing a 'scrub'. There were ten aircraft detailed from the squadron and at the original time for take-off, I think about 1830 hours, a postponement of two hours came through since there was an occlusion running north to south right through the Yorkshire and Lincolnshire airfields with cloud base down to 800 feet. At take-off time it was pouring with rain with cloud up to 16,000 feet. The occlusion was moving more slowly than forecast and a further postponement was made as the new take-off time drew near. Having hung about the messes for nearly three hours awaiting a decision no one really believed that we were going to face this weather and a great deal of incredulity was expressed when we finally found ourselves committed. One of the few nights I can remember when Harris's parentage was in doubt!

After the postponements, the ten aircraft from Pocklington started to take off at 2146 hours with the last leaving at 2206, my own aircraft, Q-Queenie, being airborne at 2147 hours.

When aircrews were tired take-offs and landings could be extremely hazardous particularly as most airfield circuits usually overlapped with one, if not two other circuits. Pocklington was no exception, with our two satellites, Melbourne and Elvington. On this night G-George, taking off at 2158 hours, seemed to have hit the slipstream from another aircraft on a nearby circuit which appeared

to have flipped it over on its back. It went straight in with the full
bomb load exploding on the edge of the town. All the crew were
killed.

Q-Queenie was the oldest, clapped out aircraft on the squadron
and from the moment we took off straight into the cloud at 700 feet
we were struggling. We were to take the northern route to Berlin
across the widest part of the North Sea to Denmark and then down
over the Baltic. Quite a lot of sea! The cloud was solid and our rate
of climb was abysmal. As we reached the Danish coast we were just
about breaking the top of the cloud at a little over 15,000 feet and
then realised that we had iced-up and the rear gunner could not see
out and half the pilot's windscreen was also covered. With the
throttles fully open we were just about able to get 135 knots IAS
instead of the usual 160. At that moment the guns from Flensburg
opened up which made us decide to turn back, although the flak was
bursting ahead of us, probably because the Germans didn't believe
anything could be flying so slow! I aimed the bombs towards the
centre of the gun flashes and we turned back for the long haul across
the North Sea, the graveyard of many aircraft. It proved to be
fortunate that our wireless operator was very experienced having
completed a previous tour on Hampdens. As a result he established
contact with base and periodically reported our progress.

We eventually landed back at base at 0312 hours and as we
reached the end of the runway had to cut the starboard outer engine
for lack of oil pressure. We proceeded to dispersal and as Dave cut
the engines the groundcrew were signalling vigorously not to open
the bomb doors as was usual. As we disembarked we were led to
first look at the port wing bomb bays where, due to icing, one of the
small bomb containers had failed to release, but as we descended to
lower temperatures had unfrozen with the result that ninety-six 4lb
incendiary bombs, all live, were now pushing through the light bomb
door. A rough landing could have set them off. It was also pointed
out that our IFF (identification friend or foe) aerial had disappeared
with the ice and the two inners of our remaining three engines were

literally pouring out their glycol coolant. Had we not turned back it would have been impossible to get back home on one good engine and we would probably have ended up in the North Sea. And so we moved into April, which was to prove our busiest month.

On 3rd April, Blackie had a cold and we were stood down. However, the wingco, George Holden, decided to go that night so, with his two gunners and the squadron navigation officer, Freddie King, conscripted me, Joe Holliday and Chiefie Beale to make up his crew. The target was Essen, which being at the heart of the Ruhr, always produced a feeling of trepidation, as it was the most heavily defended area in the Reich. We knew that we had to fly through the densest fighter belt and the heaviest flak cover to get there and then had to do it all over again to fly out.

It was 1941 hours when we became airborne, setting course shortly afterwards and climbing on track to our operational height of 17,500 feet. There were 348 Halifaxes and Lancasters due to attack that night of which fourteen made up the squadron effort. There was none of the usual chat in the aircraft which was normal with my own crew as we crossed the North Sea. Fighters were obviously active and the wingco seemed a little edgy as we flew over Holland approaching the Ruhr from the west. The weather forecast had been a bit ambiguous to the point where uncertainty of the conditions over the target caused PFF to arrange for the Oboe Mossies to drop both sky and ground markers. In the event, apart from the usual industrial haze over the area, visibility was clear. There was no sign of PFF markers as we flew east over the Ruhr and we seemed to be the only bomber on which the defences were concentrating, with flak and searchlights doing their damndest to get at us. We passed over Essen and, instead of getting the hell out of it like any sane pilot would, we continued going east with some weaving through the worst of the flak and searchlights and I expected to be coned at any time. Around Dortmund, instead of circling for a while, we turned back in for another run on Essen and it seemed to be a miracle that we were not hit. As we were passing

Essen again there was a sudden flash of colour as an Oboe prime marker exploded. I hurriedly turned the wingco on to the target and, as the aiming point lined up, thankfully pressed the bomb tit and announced, "Bombs gone". But, of course, this only covered the HE and we now had to fly straight and level for the next twelve seconds or so before I could release the incendiaries. I turned to the distributor to pull the pin out and, as I did so, realised that the arm had not moved. Immediately, I slammed the jettison bars across, letting out an expletive as I did so. The reaction from the wingco as soon as he realised that we had had a hang up was to say, "OK, we'll go round again". We then had a flaming argument over the target when I told him that procedure and the use of the jettison bars had already sent the bomb load on its way. Fred King joined in on my side as we flew out on the way home with words in the aircraft almost as hot as the flak outside.

There was quite a lot of night-fighter activity going on around us at various times and when I asked the wingco to put the aircraft into George while I took some astro shots, which he was always advocating. I was subjected to, "If you think I'm putting this blankety blank aircraft into blankety blank George until we are thirty blankety blank miles off the enemy coast, you're blankety blank mistaken. If you tell me when you're ready, I'll hold the aircraft as level as I can." We got our shots!

The squadron did not lose any aircraft that night, although John Marshall, my flight commander returned with a dead rear gunner after a run-in with a fighter. George Holden went sick the next day and was diagnosed with pleurisy from which he had suffered the previous two weeks. The word was that he had been put off all flying for the next six months, with no operational flying for twelve months. Less than three months later he superseded Guy Gibson as CO of 617 Squadron and died with all his crew on 15th September whilst attacking a viaduct on the Dortmund-Ems Canal, just one of the five lost out of the eight aircraft of 617 he led into the attack.

Back with my own crew, raids on Kiel, Frankfurt and Stuttgart followed, the latter being remembered for a directive from Harris, sent the following day to all the squadrons involved. In it we were all 'torn off a strip' for failing to hit the target. Two days later, after getting PR (photo reconnaissance) of the town, it was found that we had in fact done a fairly good job. But there was no apology!

A trip to the Skoda works at Plzen, Czechoslovakia followed on the 16th. This was another example of the discrepancy in Intelligence recording and the actual facts. We flew high on the long route to the target using astro-navigation which, from past experience, Blackie and I knew was normally accurate within three miles. The trip was fairly quiet, apart from flying near a couple of night-fighters who, apparently, did not see us. Our last fix had put us a bit to the south of the target so I was somewhat surprised to see bombing going on some miles to the south. By this time we had descended to 7,000 feet to ensure more accuracy in the bombing of an occupied country. We turned south to investigate and with some moon it soon became obvious that PFF were marking the wrong target some miles south of Plzen. I debated with Dave whether we should use the R/T to call up the other 102 aircraft, but in the end we decided against it and turned north to search for the Skoda works. With a bit of haze on the ground it was difficult to make out detail and I had to work on river configurations. I eventually found an area which resembled the layout which we bombed on a heading somewhere around 020. In fact it was open ground, as my photo later showed. After 9 hrs 41 mins in the air we landed at Pershore being a little short of fuel to enable us to get back to base. Out of 327 aircraft we lost thirty-six, a loss rate of eleven percent.

Of the fourteen from Pocklington we only lost one, from which four of the crew evaded and were back in England early in June. In spite of the above, duly reported, the Intelligence report against our name in the squadron records reads:

"Attacked primary target at 7,000 ft. 214T IAS 170. Ground haze and smoke from flares. Target believed seen in bombsight. Numerous bomb bursts from other aircraft seen. Target difficult to identify owing to glare of flares against ground haze."

The crew we had lost was our new flight commander, Squadron Leader Wally Lashbrook, who had re-formed C Flight a week earlier. He was probably the most experienced Halifax pilot in 4 Group and his loss made everyone feel mortal. If Wally could go, then none of us were fireproof!

On 20th April we took part in what was an unusual and quite exhilarating operation. Whereas earlier on in the war Bomber Command had often used moonlit nights to help locate targets, losses had risen and moonlight had since been avoided. We were, therefore, somewhat staggered to find that we were to operate with a full moon.

When we got to briefing we were more than surprised to find the target was a long trip to Stettin: and then we had one last surprise. For most of the flight we were all to fly below 700 feet, the idea being to defeat the German ground-controlled operation of their night-fighters. After take-off we climbed to 10,000 feet for safety to cross the North Sea and then, as we approached the north Danish coast dropped down to 700 feet. Up in the nose I was map-reading us across Denmark and then down over the islands of the Baltic, which looked beautiful in the moonlight. All the way the Danes were coming out of their houses to wave and flash torches at us, although the noise of about 340 four-engined aircraft passing over at such a low height must have been almost terrifying. For the crews there was little margin for error flying so low, and we were continually being buffeted by the slipstreams of other aircraft and sometimes taking avoiding action as other aircraft flashed above or across our path. For air traffic controllers of today it would have been as unbelievable as it is for aircrew of that period to understand that a 'near miss' today can take place between aircraft a mile apart. Occasionally we saw unmapped light flak ahead and would have to take evasive action. We also saw the odd unfortunate aircraft exploding as it hit the ground. On reaching a given point on the north German coast, west of Stettin, we then climbed to a bombing height of 14,000 feet. Our own attacking time was about halfway through the raid. As we approached, I remember thinking that the scene resembled a painting of an inferno with the fires from the ground tingeing the sky with crimson and with the light of the moon silhouetting our own bombers and enemy fighters weaving across the sky. For the first time I saw single-engine fighters, ME 109s and FW 190s attempting to locate targets for their guns over the target.

After bombing we turned back and dropped down to under 700 feet until we reached the west coast of Denmark and then climbed to 10,000 feet to cross the North Sea. Altogether quite different from our normal raids, although out of the sixteen aircraft put up by the squadron we lost two.

After losing our flight commander on Plzen, he had now been replaced by Squadron Leader J. Flowerdew, a peacetime officer who had spent most of his time in training. In the last four days of April we put in three more trips, the first back to the hell of the Ruhr in the shape of Duisburg. We were at 18,000 feet and on arrival there was 5/10ths cloud at about 1,000 feet and no markers, which meant an orbit of the target before we were able to locate the river and markers to bomb. Unfortunately, although most of our bomb load went down, after leaving the target, we found that we had had a hang up of two 1,000lb HEs. This was one of those things that sometimes happened for which there was no explanation, so on our way back over the North Sea we jettisoned them manually in case they fell off when we landed. We lost one aircraft from the squadron which went down in the sea off Texel. I still often wonder whether anyone has ever totalled how many Bomber Command aircraft were lost in the North Sea.

Two days later we did a Gardening trip, the code name for mine-laying, although it sounds more like a euphemism. We had to drop 1,500lb mines with very sophisticated fuses in the Kattegat. Every squadron had a naval officer attached to it who was responsible for overseeing the settings and recording where the mines were dropped. After all, the navy might, at some time in the future, have to clear the mine fields. The usual procedure, as was carried out that night, was to come down to 1,500 feet, pinpoint a landmark and then carry out a timed run from that point. Sounds quite safe but the Germans had quite a number of heavily-armed flakships around the coast and it was easy to run into one without warning. At the low height, even at night, it was easy pickings. However, the visibility was good, with a cloud base about five hundred feet above us, so we were in and out without any problems. This was probably the heaviest mine-laying operation of the war but we suffered badly, losing twenty-two aircraft, over ten percent of the 207 employed. However, there was always a good return of sunken German shipping as the result of Bomber Command mine-laying.

On the last day of April, our hearts sank as we found ourselves briefed to attack Essen once more. Right in the heart of the Ruhr, that name always evoked a sense of foreboding as one faced the prospect of battling in and out through the miles of searchlights and AA guns protecting it after flying 250 miles through the night-fighter belt. We took off at 2347 hours and climbed to 19,000 feet where we found ourselves above 10/10ths cloud. This had been predicted and the Oboe Mosquito markers were prepared with sky-marking flares. When we arrived over the target there was a gap in the clouds and we were able to confirm accuracy of markers. Landing after five o'clock in the morning it was more or less breakfast time as we crawled into bed.

Since the middle of April we'd had our own brand new aircraft, X-X ray, which gave a very good performance. However we now had leave due to us which meant surrendering the aircraft to the tender mercies of other crews while we were away. Before going we uttered dire threats to other crews in C Flight who might misuse our aircraft in our absence. When we returned, it was to find that we had lost another flight commander, Squadron Leader Flowerdew only having survived one operation. It seemed almost as though there was a jinx on C Flight commanders (two in three weeks, both being lost on their second operation), so Johnnie Marshall of B Flight moved over to stop the rot. We had been in B Flight back in February when we joined the squadron, so he was no stranger.

For the next week or so there was a lull in Bomber Command activity which was rather mystifying and we counted nine days with no operations. Then on the 23rd May, clarity came and it seemed that we were on a maximum effort with twenty-two aircraft being bombed up for the night. This would be our twentieth operation as a crew although our first with Jim Nightingale, who was replacing our former wireless operator Norman Beale, who had previously done a first tour in 5 Group. After our last operation he had been called to the adjutant's office and told that as he had completed fifty operations he was now 'screened' and would not do any more ops. So we had had to find ourselves another one. Jim Nightingale was an experienced wireless operator who had lost his crew one night when he was unable to fly with them. This was to be his first trip with his new permanent crew.

Like most crews who managed to survive we were very close-knit, very rarely being off the station unless we were all together and taking it rather hard that Chiefie had been taken away from us without a 'by your leave'. We had our own crew song adapted from that well-known ditty 'Sweet Violets' which had been sung to distraction in pub after pub since we had joined the squadron at the beginning of the year. Having a rear gunner from Dublin and a mid-upper from Belfast often led to interesting arguments when flying on the long grind to Holland or Denmark over the North Sea when life might have been quiet and otherwise dull.

When we got to the briefing room and the target was revealed there were the usual curses and trepidation at finding ourselves back on the 'Happy Valley' run but, as a crew, we couldn't complain since we had not operated since April, when we had admittedly had a heavy month. This was the March/July period which was later to be known as the Battle of the Ruhr. As the briefing commenced we quickly found out that this was to be something different: the heaviest raid of the war. Up to this date, apart from the thousand bomber raids of 1942 which pressed everything into service which could take off, without necessarily being able to carry much bomb load, Bomber Command had only been able to send between 300 and 580 aircraft on individual raids. Tonight Dortmund was to suffer the mightiest blow that the Command could administer with the use of 826 aircraft, the majority being 'heavies'; Lancasters, Halifaxes and Stirlings with 151 Wellingtons and thirteen Oboe marking Mosquitoes. This was presumably why Command had not operated for the previous nine days in order to get as many aircraft as possible serviceable.

The weather forecast was good, with no cloud cover over the target, and at the duly appointed time (2325 hours) we took off and headed towards Holland. We usually expected to meet fighters some thirty miles off the enemy coast which thereafter continued to make life difficult with the help of various flak and searchlight batteries dotted all over the place until we began to close in on the Ruhr. At that period, as bombers approached the Ruhr the game changed. Masses of searchlights and guns took over. It was estimated at that time that the Ruhr was protected by several thousand AA guns and to meet them on your own was never a pleasant prospect. Again, as with fighters, if within the stream, it was difficult for the guns and searchlights to use radar to predict individual aircraft and so, once a raid got into its stride the flak became more of a barrage which had to be flown through, rather than suffering direct fire on individual aircraft. For Pathfinders and aircraft in the van of the attack those early minutes of the raid were the most dangerous as the guns and searchlights had the opportunity to pick up individual bombers and send up very accurate predicted fire and always took the most of their chances. Anyone flying straight and level for more than a few seconds on their own could be certain of some near misses, if not direct hits. Because of their role in marking the target PFF losses of heavies were very high at this stage since they had to follow in the Oboe Mosquitoes, which flew very much higher, and put down continuous back-up markers on the aiming point. By this time, there had been another pair of Oboe control stations installed which meant that marking by Oboe could be carried out every five minutes providing the equipment in the aircraft did not fail. Oboe had proved to be the only reliable and extremely accurate marking system to overcome the notorious mist and smoke cover which had for so long prevented Command from hitting the Ruhr and, therefore, since March it had been a cardinal rule that bombing on the Ruhr only commenced with the laying of an Oboe marker. It was then the job of the PFF back-up heavies to maintain continuity of the markers by aiming theirs, of a different colour, at the Oboe ones. This ensured that if there was a failure in an Oboe Mossie later in the attack the aiming point would still be marked, although not quite so accurately.

On this night Halifaxes of 4 Group were leading the attack with my squadron in the van. We had had an uneventful trip so far, crossing the North Sea and Holland without problems despite having observed aircraft falling on either side of us. We continued across Germany before we turned on our final leg which would bring us to Dortmund from the north. As we started to run down to the Ruhr the flak began to warm up and turned into the usual flashes and thumps so familiar to anyone who has experienced AA fire, quite frightening in its way. I checked the latest wind with Blackie and, after switching on, fed this into the bombsight before checking that all the switches were on, to ensure the bombs were live and the distributor would function. Taking the bomb tit release button in my hand I settled down in the prone position over the bombsight ready to carry out my task.

Everything was still dark, although a clear starry night with very good visibility, and as we neared our target the flak intensified although, as I recollect, there were at this point no searchlights. Quite often the Germans would delay the use of these until the target had been marked in case, one presumes, the searchlights would give them away. Being in the forefront of the attack we kept on our course to Dortmund although we were only a couple of minutes from our ETA, and no markers were yet visible. Suddenly, a vivid splash of colour appeared ahead and below us and relief set in that this was the primary Oboe marker and we would not have to 'go round again'.

Dave, operating the controls, called out "Bomb doors open ... bomb doors open". I took over and guided Dave through my bomb-sight, "Left ... left ... steady .... steady ... right ... steady ... stead..y ... left, left ... steady, stead..y .... bombs gone". I pressed the tit and the aircraft jumped with the release of the two 1,000lb high explosives. At the same time the photoflash left its 'chute at the rear of the aircraft and we now flew straight and level while I counted out the prescribed number of seconds. We carried a mixed load of HE and incendiary bombs which unfortunately had different terminal velocities. This meant that the high explosive bombs had a better forward travel than the smaller incendiaries which would fall almost vertically. We still, therefore, had six small bomb containers of eight 30lb incendiaries and seven SBCs of ninety 4lb incendiaries to be dropped. These would be released in sequence so that the hundreds of incendiaries would cover an area over a hundred yards long. The idea was that the HE should open up the buildings and then the incendiaries follow to set fire to the exposed rubble. In order for this to happen there had to be a time lag between dropping the two types of bombs. Hence the timed run. The bomb release had also set up the camera ready to record our position at the time of impact of the bombs. Providing we maintained our run which went on for a little longer after the release of the incendiaries the centre of the photograph would, as I've noted earlier, indicate the impact point of our bomb load. It was not often that I had a virgin target to aim at with no other bombing except the Oboe marker. But, of course, this meant that we were way out front, an ideal target for the gunners below and, moreover, making life easy for them with the prolonged straight and level photo run. We had been getting a bumpy ride as the flak intensified almost to the point of realisation of the old line shoot 'The flak was so heavy you could get out and walk on it'.

With the bomb doors closed we continued to cross the target going south and had just got our photo and were now free to jinx about a bit to confuse the guns when there was an almighty bang. The aircraft almost shuddered to a stop and we seemed to be dropping out of the sky. There was confusion on the intercom which had gone extremely fuzzy with the loss of the generator and, for a brief moment, there was a babel of voices as all the crew were enquiring what had happened. The rear gunner's voice continued and Dave cut in to ask, "Who's that?" "It's me, the rear gunner, what's up Dave?" The answer was very swift, "Prepare to bale out".

With the loss of power the aircraft had swung to starboard and as we rapidly descended we were heading west along the Ruhr valley with all the gunners turning their fire on us and searchlights seeking us out for the kill. Meanwhile, in the nose, Blackie and I clipped on our 'chutes and started to clear the navigator's chair away from the forward escape hatch. From the first time I had seen the Ruhr being bombed I had made up my mind that I would never bale out over a German target on the assumption that the populace would be quite likely to tear aircrew to bits – and in fact this did happen in many instances, sometimes observed by their fellow crew members. And here we were, falling out of the sky over the Ruhr, of all places. To this day, I am not sure whether I would have jumped in those circumstances. All these thoughts were to be re-enacted a year later when I did have to jump but, fortunately, not in the target area. However, Dave was still wrestling with the controls and attempting to reduce our rate of descent. In the meantime, Joe had decided that maybe the petrol tanks had been holed and, although he had, as normal, changed to full tanks before going in to the target he hurriedly turned the cocks to switch to alternative tanks. By this time we were coned in the searchlights and were down from 17,000 to 7,000 feet with everything that was within reach beginning to bear on us. This now included light ack-ack with the frightening tracer, every one of which seemed to be heading towards the aircraft before it curled away. While all this was happening, I had looked back towards the cockpit and had been surprised to see a pair of white socked feet dancing by the side of the pilot. At the time I did not question what they were doing there and it was not until many years later when talking to Dave that I recalled the incident and asked for an explanation. Apparently, on the order "prepare to bale out", Andy had shot out of his turret, his boots being ripped off as he scrambled out, and ran up the fuselage to the cockpit where he then shouted in Dave's ear words to the effect of "Come on Dave, this can't happen to us, you can't let it happen to us. Get it flying again, *it can't happen to us.*" But then, so many crews believed that it couldn't happen to them, only to other crews!

At 7,000 feet, the miracle occurred as gradually the engines began to splutter again and Dave began to stabilise the aircraft. With power to our elbow, as it were, we now had a chance against the enemy, weaving to get out of the searchlights and, above all, starting to climb to get some height again, having lost some 10,000 feet in our fall. As we were in the middle of the Ruhr we had no choice but to continue to fly westward through the best defended area in Germany but we eventually made our way out and had an uneventful trip back to base.

Arriving back at dispersal we now had the chance to examine the aircraft to see what had happened. We had apparently been hit by shrapnel from a rather near miss, as witnessed by some twenty plus holes in the aircraft, with one large piece slicing through the fire extinguisher buttons, setting them off in three engines, and thus giving them foam rather than fuel to digest. Not taking kindly to this, they gave up. We lost thirty-eight aircraft that night, but it could easily have been thirty-nine. That same night, and again, just after dropping its bombs a Wellington of 431 Squadron was also hit and the pilot and rear gunner baled out thinking the tail had been lost, leaving a friend of mine, with whom I had trained in South Africa, trapped with the navigator and wireless operator in the nose. Sergeant Stu Sloan, an observer cum bomb aimer like me, regained control of the aircraft with the help of the other two and in spite of two very rough engines one of which had to be shut down, not only managed to fly the Wellington back to this country but landed it for good measure. He was given an immediate award of the CGM, commissioned in the field and sent on a pilot's course. Without his efforts it could have been forty lost that night.

But to return to our base in Yorkshire. The following morning it was arranged for us to meet up with an engineering officer for an inspection of our aircraft. When we got to dispersal we found him already wandering around, poking into holes at various places as engineers are wont to do. For a few minutes we all drifted around surveying the damage before we assembled in front of the Halifax with the engineer facing us but keeping a few paces distance from us. Then began an encounter that will last in my memory until I die.

The officer concerned had been a regular NCO in the inter-war years when all actions had to be governed by a book of rules. He first addressed Dave by asking for an account of the events of the previous night. This Dave gave in full, answering questions as he went. There was a brief pause before the following duologue took place:

Eng. Off: "How far can a Halifax fly on one engine?"
Dave: "Not very far."
E.O.:   "Could you have flown back from the Ruhr on one."
Dave: "That would be impossible."
E.O.:   "You would agree that three fire extinguishers have been operated."
Dave: "Yes."
E.O.:   "What are the regulations about using an

engine after the fire extinguisher has been used?"

Dave:　"Normally, shut down the engine, feather the propeller, and don't use again, but this was different. The engines had not been on fire."

E.O.:　"The book says that an engine must not be used again after the fire extinguisher has been used. Three of them have been operated therefore you could not have used those engines again. A Halifax could not have flown back from the Ruhr on one engine. It just couldn't have happened, otherwise you wouldn't be here."

We stood there dumbfounded. Apparently, we weren't where we thought we were. There was not the slightest sign of a smile on his face or humour in the situation as he turned away and arranged for our aircraft to have three engines changed and the holes to be patched up. At the tender age of twenty I had learnt that, when using a rule book, always make sure that it was up-to-date and applied to the current situation before using it.

When later that morning I visited the photographic section it was with great satisfaction that I found my developed photo showing a very clear picture of Dortmund with the aiming point right bang in the centre. At least I knew where I had been, even if I didn't know where I was!

Chapter V

Halifax Down!

About twenty-four hours later on 25th May we had our aircraft back with three replacement engines and all the holes repaired and were ready for ops again, this time to Dusseldorf. Although there were 759 aircraft attacking, the target was covered in heavy cloud at such a height that all the marker flares were lost in the clouds and we had to bomb on ETA. Not very satisfactory for the loss of thirty-seven aircraft and crews with very little damage inflicted on the enemy.

At this time it had become policy in Bomber Command not to operate during full moon periods to avoid unsustainable losses, so, for the first ten days of June no major raids were mounted. Dave Hewlett's commission came through at the end of May which meant that he went off for a few days commissioning leave. On his return we did a bit of bombing and gunnery practice as well as some formation flying before, on 11th June we were detailed to attack Dusseldorf again. Harris was nothing if not persistent! This time we went with 780-odd aircraft. The target did have a small amount of cloud cover but not sufficient to save it. The Oboe Mossies had come prepared for all conditions so that, as we went in at 16,000 feet, we had target indicator sky markers bursting above us and at our own height. I had some trouble with the sighting head gyro of the bombsight but managed to get the bombs away on target twenty-one minutes into the attack. German accounts record forty-two industries being put out of production with some thirty-odd others being badly affected and twenty military installations hit. There were also over 8,000 major fires burning when we left.

The next night we were again detailed for the Ruhr, this time Bochum with an all four-engine attack of Lancasters and Halifaxes, some 492 aircraft. In the event it was not a pleasant trip as, when we reached operational height of 19,000 feet and were flying in a route from the north of the target, the Northern Lights went into full production and lit up the sky on our port, while to the south we had a waning moon. So we were fairly well illuminated for the night-fighters, particularly as we were flying over 10/10th cloud cover below. Constantly we saw aircraft blowing up to our port and starboard and I was rather surprised to find on return that we had only lost twenty-four aircraft, albeit about one in twenty, including one from 102 Squadron. I had always looked forward to seeing the Northern Lights and they were a great spectacle, but we could have done without them. The flak was, as usual, intensive, to the point that Blackie was lucky that night as one chunk of shrapnel tore past him, missing by an inch or so. Had he not had his head down over his chart at the time he would surely have died that night or, at least, received serious injury. We bombed on sky markers which were extremely accurate and left Bochum devastated, landing back at base just after four in the morning after five hours in the air.

For a week we had no aircraft operating and then, on the 19th June, we were detailed to attack the Schneider armanent plant at Le Creusot in France. It was a maximum effort for the squadron and we were to put up twenty-three aircraft out of the 290 Halifaxes and Stirlings on the raid. With a friendly occupied country it was always necessary to take particular care to ensure that bombs did not fall on housing areas. On our way across France we were accompanied at one stage by a couple of German night-fighters but, fortunately, while we watched them carefully, they seemed to be unaware of our presence. The weather forecast was clear and we were scheduled early in the attack, which was to be carried out on an individual basis by crews, identifying the factory by flares to be laid by the Pathfinders and bombing at their discretion. We arrived with no cloud and good visibility, enabling me to identify a nearby lake from

7,500 feet and so locate the Scheider works with no trouble. We bombed on a heading of 050°M at an indicated airspeed of 190 knots and I watched my bombs, with others, striking the buildings. Unfortunately, heavy smoke clouds developed and later aircraft dropped their bombs on the nearby housing estate.

Although in France, Le Creusot was at a somewhat longer range than Berlin from our base in Yorkshire and so after over seven hours in the air we landed at Tangmere near the south coast due to fuel shortage, Command having dictated that, in order to carry maximum bomb load, we would not carry overloaded fuel tanks. Being in the early hours of the morning we had breakfast and snatched a few hours sleep before taking off and returning north to Pocklington. There, we were greeted with the news that the next day our secondment to the Intensive Flying Development Flight at RAF Boscombe Down for five weeks had been ordered and we must be ready to leave the next morning.

On the 21st June, a Transport Command Harrow landed to take us along to Boscombe Down together with some nominated ground-crew. On the way we dropped into Elvington, one of our satellite airfields housing 77 Squadron, to pick up another experienced crew to join us. I must admit it was not an ideal occasion to take groundcrew on what, for most of them, was their maiden flight. The Harrow was a high wing monoplane not exactly known for stability in bumpy conditions. And the conditions were just that on the warm June day with plenty of cumulus cloud building up, under which we were flying. The fuselage fittings were not exactly made for creature comfort, consisting mainly of wooden benches running fore and aft and it was not long before the ground lads were making a beeline for the funnel and tube at the rear of the fuselage. I think it was the only time I had ever come near to feeling sick in flight, as the smell of vomit permeated the aircraft, leaving me thankful as we landed and I was able to leave the aircraft.

We reported to the Intensive Flying Development Flight on arrival at Boscombe Down to discover that our job was to carry out 150 hours flying on the Halifax Mark III prototype. This particular aircraft had been put together from the oldest Halifax airframe and consequently we suffered continually from servicing problems. It was six days before we had the opportunity to get the aircraft off the ground. When we did, it was a revelation. The tail units had been modified and, after the Merlins, the feel of the Bristol Hercules engines was phenomenal as we literally powered off the airfield with the air speed indicator trying to keep up. After that taster it was three weeks before the aircraft was fit to take to the air again. Boscombe Down was a highly secret testing and experimental station for all new RAF aircraft before they went into service. The contour of the airfield was rather like a saucer with no runways and when travelling round the perimeter track one was constantly taken by surprise as aircraft took off and literally came up out of the ground to pass overhead. The tannoy was in constant use warning of low level aircraft doing speed trials across the airfield for which 'low level' really did mean low level. Another hazard was guard dogs. These were used for patrol of the establishment at night but, somehow, had a habit of getting loose during the day. As a result, it was quite the norm to have warnings over the tannoy about dogs on the loose, usually Irish wolfhounds, and to "stand still if approached". Nearly all our flying was carried out in daylight but one day we arrived back as dusk was falling and by the time we had parked the aircraft it was beginning to get quite dark. We rang from the Flights for transport and waited. And waited. We couldn't ring again because we had locked the door of the flight office and did not have a key. It was about an hour before the transport turned up. It was a small canvas covered truck and on her way the WAAF had been waylaid by a dog which had jumped on the back and menaced her to the point where she had to stop and just wait. There were no mobiles in those days!

In the second week of August our flying in the prototype almost culminated in disaster during a hairy cross-country trip. We were flying north to Edinburgh with a full dummy war load and, after about an hour, the inner starboard engine gave up with a bang and we, therefore, had to feather it with the cowling flapping about a bit. We continued with our flight until, near Newcastle, one of the port engines began to show low oil pressure requiring a second engine to be feathered. Now, with only two good engines left, we turned south to get back to Boscombe Down, it not being the done thing to 'land away' from the experimental base with a prototype aircraft. (We had previously done that, landing at Pocklington when we had smelled burning rubber from an electrical fault which took two days to right. Even so, Dave got hauled over the coals for landing away.) We made good progress on two engines until the second port engine started to overheat as we reached the Oxford area and so, for the remainder of the flight, Dave used the two port engines alternately with the starboard outer to reach Boscombe, switching them both in to use for a three-engine landing. Upon inspecting the aircraft we found one of the pistons of the starboard engine had come adrift and the resultant shuddering seemed to have caused a lot of the airframe rivets, particularly in the starboard wing and fuselage, to have parted, which made the aircraft unserviceable. Two weeks later we were able to take it up on an air test and pronounce it fit to fly again. After a few more trips we flew it up to Pocklington for three days to give some of the 4 Group pilots a taste of handling the Mk III.

Since leaving Pocklington in June my commission had come through and at the end of August I flew back to base to take my commissioning leave. Upon returning to Boscombe, I found the prototype was still unserviceable and on 13th September we flew it back to the Handley-Page works at Radlett and returned in a Warwick to await one of the first two production models of the Halifax III on which to carry out the necessary development flying.

Within forty-eight hours the aircraft had arrived at IFDF and, with it, the boss of Boscombe Down, Group Captain Purvis, a remarkable and competent pilot. It was he who had been scheduled to fly the Spitfire in an attempt on the world air speed record in 1937. This was pulled as the Air Ministry did not wish to disclose its performance to our potential enemies. It was believed that he had force-landed aircraft some twenty-one times without damage and the 22nd took place while we were at Boscombe, being the first time he had damaged an aircraft. Group Captain Purvis decided on 16th September to take up our new Halifax himself, and I was to go with him, on an air test flight. In Britain during the war there were a number of industrial areas protected by balloons known as prohibited areas over which one did not knowingly fly, for obvious reasons. Some AA batteries in these areas were also a little trigger happy. Near to Boscombe Down was Southampton, a prohibited area. We took off and cruised around for a while doing climbs and various other tests, after which I became aware that we were whizzing past balloon cables in the Southampton area. I could hardly assume that on such a clear day the group captain did not know where he was but, nevertheless, felt that I could not stay silent. After all, he might be testing out the competence of this newly created officer sitting alongside him. I piped up and, as tactfully as I could, pointed out that we were over a prohibited area and that the cables were getting a bit denser. The reply came back immediately and almost apologetically, "It's OK, I'm just testing for manoeuvrability". It was the first and last time I ever flew into a balloon barrage.

In tandem with the 77 Squadron crew, we then went on to record the fastest time for a multi-engined aircraft to complete a 150 hour programme of development flying, such was the quality of the aircraft. We completed by 22nd October and then went on leave. As a result of the original problems, the five week secondment had became nearly five months after which we were flown back to Pocklington by Group Captain Purvis in a Lancaster. Back at base, our crew was screened as having completed our tour and Dave was required to convert pilots on squadrons re-equipping with the Halifax IIIs. Within limits, I was given the choice of where I wanted to go. Knowing quite a few of the instructors, including Chiefie Beale and the bombing leader, Eric Hargreaves, at Rufforth I opted to go as a bombing instructor to 1663 HCU Rufforth. Navigators and bomb aimers were of the same genesis and at Rufforth were in adjacent offices which made for a chummy atmosphere and, not surprisingly, for combined drinking operations at the Half Moon and the Hole in the Wall in nearby York. Invariably Jim Lewis and I could be found at these gatherings and it was as a result of this that I was to volunteer when he was looking for a bomb aimer to team up with his crew on his second tour.

* * *

There is no doubt that whatever the skill or experience of a bomber crew, at the end of the day Lady Luck inevitably had the last say. A random shell or fighter in the right place would negate all the skills of the group of aircrew who had joined together to become one. To some extent aircrew had the opportunity to decide their own destiny in that they themselves, in most cases, chose with whom they would crew up. Even so, one can often trace a string of circumstances which led to a single event.

In May 1943 Stan Somerscales completed his first operational tour with 10 Squadron at Melbourne and he and his crew split up to act as instructors at various training units. He and Jim Lewis, the navigator, were posted to 1663 Heavy Conversion Unit at Rufforth together with the wireless operator, Jack Reavill, and the engineer, Sid Stephen. The rest of the crew went to other stations. It was at Rufforth that Stan worked with Hank Iveson who was one of the flight commanders at the heavy conversion unit, having previously flown operationally with 76 Squadron.

The countdown to the events of 22/23 April 1944 began just after I was posted to Rufforth at the end of November 1943. A week or so before Christmas Hank Iveson was promoted to wing commander and went off to Holme-on-Spalding Moor to lead 76 Squadron. When vacancies occurred for flight commanders, where else had he to look but to Rufforth, to those officers whom he had had the opportunity to assess; first Kenny Clack and then, the last week in March, Stan Somerscales.

Ideally, Stan would have wished to reassemble all his original crew but neither his gunners nor bomb aimer were available so he had to look elsewhere. Two gunners, John Rowe and Harry Poole came down from Driffield where they had been instructors at the survival school which was located there. John had carried out his first tour on 76 Squadron when it was commanded by Cheshire and Harry's first tour had been completed in another bomber group on Lancasters. The question of a bomb aimer was left almost to the end but, when the original member of Stan's crew was not forthcoming, he and Jim came with all sweetness to the bombing section looking for a volunteer. Being somewhat bored with instruction and with a view to once again enjoying squadron life, I did not need much persuasion; and so the die was cast.

RAF Holme-on-Spalding Moor, the home of 76 Squadron from June 1943 on, was a bleak wartime airfield with very few comforts, just south of Market Weighton on the York-Hull road, and it was here that, as Stan's crew, we started to settle in with our posting there on 28th March. A few days followed in getting acquainted with the station and squadron routine as well as the Halifax III, before pushing off for seven days' leave prior to operations. This gave a few days to get over the shock of the loss of Kenny Clack, one of the flight commanders whom we had known at Rufforth, together with two other crews on the Nuremburg raid of 30th March.

It was arranged that the squadron commander would share an aircraft with Stan Somerscales who was A Flight commander and on return from leave we carried out two raids on railway marshalling yards at Ottignies and Tergnier. Then a new aircraft came on the strength which the ATA pilot considered the best Halifax she had ever flown. Nominated I-Ink, the wingco decided to take it on its baptism of fire at the first available opportunity. So on the 22nd April his name went on the battle order and our crew were stood down; but this state of affairs was to change as the telephone began to buzz between Heslington Hall (4 Group HQ) and Holme-on-Spalding. The CO had 'forgotten' that he had completed his quota for the month and was being reminded of this oversight by Group. For an hour or so calls went backwards and forwards between Hank Iveson and Group with our crew hovering around waiting for the decision as to whether we were go or not. Eventually, as Stan and I sat in the office with the CO, there was another phone call. Hank picked up the phone announced himself and said nothing more until he put the phone down. Then, "That was the AOC, (AVM Carr). He just said, 'Hank, you're not flying tonight: that's an order' and put the phone down on me". And so, for Stan and the rest of us, it was go.

The target was Dusseldorf within the area designated the Ruhr or, in Bomber Command parlance, 'Happy Valley'. It was well-known to our crew who had all been involved in what has since been termed "The Battle of the Ruhr" in the first half of 1943. Briefing followed the pattern that had become all too familiar since starting operations. The Ruhr always produced apprehension even in the most seasoned veteran and tonight was no exception. I had been there ten times before in the early months of the previous year and losses sustained during that period had been some of the heaviest of the war. The route was always a matter of great interest and tonight the coloured string on the wall map took us down to the south coast and then east across northern France before swinging north-east at the last moment over Belgium and south-east Holland to reach Dusseldorf. Two other major operations and a spoof raid were also being mounted to keep the German defences guessing: in all, over 1,100 aircraft would be attacking. The met officer had good clear weather to offer and he was followed by navigation, bombing and W/T briefings. The intelligence officer sounded off on the latest information available on enemy defences before Hank Iveson finally rounded off the briefing with a few well-chosen words.

We drifted out of the briefing room and went about our various tasks in preparing for the night before spending the last hour or so stretched out on a bed. As usual, at the appointed hour we made our way to the mess for an operational supper of bacon and egg, afterwards filling our flasks with hot coffee, before making our way to the crew room. The routine continued; turn out pockets, removing all forms of identification, put on flying boots, mae west and harness, collect parachutes and rations, codes, 'colours of the day' signal cartridges and anything else required, before moving out to the waiting bus which was to transport us to our aircraft a mile or so away around the perimeter track at dispersal.

We were somewhat quieter than we had been some twenty-four hours earlier in the Half Moon at York. Jim Lewis had a Morris 8 open four-seater but somehow it always managed to carry five or six. During the time we were in the Half Moon several members of the crew had telephoned home to tell their folk to look out for our photographs which were due to appear in the *Daily Press*. The previous night, on our return from a raid on the railway yards at Ottignies, photographers and reporters from a press agency had been visiting 76 Squadron and, as the most experienced crew on the squadron we had been interviewed and photographed leaving our aircraft. Unfortunately, possibly because we subsequently went 'missing', no trace of these pictures was ever found. So we were celebrating in good style and had a rumbustuous ride back to Holme. Pride, literally, doth go before a fall!

At dispersal we climbed into the Halifax, stowed parachutes and other equipment before carrying out last minute checks. A final smoke in the cold night air and then all in again as time arrived for start-up. Each of the four engines in turn roared into life and, after warming up, were checked for magneto drop to minimise the risk of engine cut out during take-off. Slowly we moved out of dispersal in the inky darkness on to the perimeter track in order to wend our way round to the end of the runway, there to take our turn for take-off with the rest of 76 Squadron, some twenty-two aircraft in all.

We lifted off at 2236 hours in clear conditions with no moon and settled down to the slow climb with full bomb load to the operational height of 19,000 feet. Very little conversation took place on the intercom other than routine chat between Jim Lewis and the skipper and comments by the gunners on other nearby aircraft. The usual thoughts passed through the mind as we crossed the English coastline. Open seas were always viewed as a potential grave. God knows how many bomber boys were swallowed up by them. However, tonight was a short sea crossing and it was not long before I was reporting, "enemy coast ahead".

On we roared with everything around us completely obscured by the blackness of the night except for the stars above. It could be said that, apart from the odd bit of AA fire witnessed as some poor aircraft strayed, the flight was rather quiet, if one ignored the thumping drone of the four Hercules engines. Occasionally, we were reassured that we were not alone by a bump as we hit the slipstream of another bomber. There was little sign of enemy activity as the aircraft reached the end of our easterly course and Jim gave Stan the northerly course for the last leg of our approach to Dusseldorf, tracking across the east of Belgium and Holland. Flying with Dave Hewlett on 102, I had been used to weaving our way through the fighter belt, so was a little unhappy that Stan was flying a rigid straight and level course as the Halifax crossed Belgium and began to move up Holland between Maastricht and Aachen. All was quiet with no sign of the enemy, but I resolved to have a word with Stan on our return. Suddenly there was a muffled thud and at least three voices, including the skipper's and Sid Stephen's, cried out, "What was that?" For a very short period of just two seconds or so there was complete silence. Then, "The wing's on fire!" This from Harry Poole, the mid-upper. Again, the following silence was quickly shattered by Stan's order, "Bale out!" It was an order on which he had not had to agonize. A fire in an engine or in the fuselage might be dealt with by fire extinguishers, but a wing, that was a different matter. With hundreds of gallons of high octane petrol in each wing it does not need too much imagination to visualize the inevitable end.

In order to give Stan a lighter aircraft I jettisoned the bomb load, hoping to make the aircraft easier to handle whilst everyone got out.

That done, I threw off my oxygen mask and helmet, clipped on my parachute and turned to help Jim Lewis remove the escape hatch beneath the seat where he had recently been sitting. Being new, the hatch was proving troublesome but the combined effort of the two of us quickly overcame the problem and we dropped the hatch door out into the night.

Jim Lewis was the first out of the stricken aircraft with my assistance. A tall thick-set Herefordshire farmer, Jim squeezed through the dark hole and, with a helpful push from me, dropped away into the blackness below as I wished him "Good luck".

Having seen Jim on his way, I crouched by the hatch reluctant to follow him. This sort of thing didn't happen to us, only to other people. There was almost a dreamlike quality to the whole thing. It had happened so quickly, no anti-aircraft fire; no apparent night-fighter attack; nothing against which we could have taken action to produce a fighting chance.

As I lay there, my mind went back to less than a year ago when I was with my first crew and we were falling out of the sky over Dortmund; we had got away then, so I was a rather reluctant candidate for a drop into the unknown. Was there a possibility of the fire going out? Various other thoughts went through my mind as, laying there in the dark, I debated the matter with myself. I stretched out and looked back up into the cockpit. Jack Reavill was standing there with his parachute on and had another one in his hands which he was trying to clip to Stan's harness. Behind him was a faint red glow and smoke was drifting in from the fuselage. It was time to go! How much time had passed since I had discarded my helmet and oxygen was of academic interest. Maybe a minute or so but as I dropped through the hatch I felt a bit muzzy and so I almost immediately pulled the rip-cord. The last thing I remember was the black bulk of the port wing above, and then, nothing, until I awoke on the ground.

Chapter VI

A Serious Headache

The rising sun, therefore, found me just inside the woods on a hill overlooking a village which lay about 400 yards below. This, I was to find out many years later, was Teuven, a village in Belgium; so apparently in my ignorance I had crossed the Dutch/Belgian border during the night. But this I was not to know at the time. During the day woodcutters to the north of me could be heard talking and calling to each other but to an inexperienced ear the voices sounded rather Germanic which made for a feeling of insecurity. On the other hand the sound of people from below there did appear to have a French flavour. The day passed very slowly and I began to realise that I had not travelled very far from where I had baled out. This next evening more distance must be covered and then perhaps it might be possible to seek help.

As darkness fell, leaving the cover of the woods I trekked down the hill keeping to the east of the village. The weather during the two days since my arrival had been fine and sunny but now things took a turn for the worse. The skies clouded over and the night became pitch black. One literally could not see the proverbial hand in front of the face. Then it rained, bucketsful, followed by thunder and lightning, to make it the most miserable and terrifying night I had ever suffered in twenty-one years of life. Within a few seconds I was soaked through and, being in open country, decided to make my way to the village and shelter in the church porch. With the conditions, this was not so easy to carry out and while crossing a fence in the darkness I stumbled against a low hut which seemed ideal in which to take cover.

The rain was still falling out of the skies and the thunder and lightning was of an intensity I had never before experienced. The hut had no door and, making to go inside, it became obvious that I was not alone. What looked comfortable in the dark was actually a pig-sty and the pigs were not taking kindly either to the thunder or my presence. As a Londoner, pigs had not been within the compass of standard education and the present circumstances did not seem ripe for this to be corrected. With a couple of swine nosing against my legs I turned tail and with some surprise bumped into a dead tree stump standing about four feet high. With a great deal of relief I perched myself on the top and would have sung like a nightingale except that things were not really improving. The storm was intensifying, the night became blacker, and the pigs seemed determined to assault the tree stump as another noise developed, this time, man-made. Overhead, the roar of four-engine bombers grew, as a very large force destined for Germany passed overhead. Coupled with this was the staccato bursts of cannon and machine-gun fire as an air battle took place directly overhead. Almost immediately a bomber blew up and the cloud above was hit by a red glow as the doomed aircraft fell to earth a mile or so away to the south with a further explosion. The storm continued unabated, with torrential rain, and sitting on my perch was like being in a bath with the shower going full pelt. Gradually, the roar of the aircraft faded and as the night wore on the storm subsided and, with the village nearby, it now seemed sensible to seek help, or at least a change of clothing, if I was to stay fit and healthy.

Dawn came as I waited at the edge of the village for some sign of life and the opportunity to weigh up any potential help before breaking cover. At about 6:00 a.m. there was a bleating of sheep and a woman appeared from the back of one of the cottages driving a small flock towards the fields where I waited. Taking a chance that we would be alone, I walked towards her and, being without any French or Flemish, tried to convey in English and sign language that I wanted to get rid of my RAF uniform and had she any clothes I could have. It seemed to take an age for her to understand but suddenly the penny dropped as she associated me with the crashed aircraft of the night before. Grasping my arm and abandoning her sheep she quickly hurried me back to her cottage, through the front door, where I was introduced to three other Belgians, presumably her husband and two sons. The problem of communication was still with me as we had no common language and they were obviously suspicious to the point that I did not know whether I was going to get help, be sent on my way, or handed over to the Germans. One of the men, taking instruction from the others, had left the house shortly after my arrival but it was to be thirty-three years later before I learnt the full story.

My entry into the village had been observed by a Dutch policeman, Herman Ankoné, who had been attending a wedding the previous day in this Belgian village of Teuven. The celebrations having continued till late after curfew, he had stayed overnight in the house opposite to the one I had contacted and, getting up early in order to return to duty the other side of the border, had observed me entering the village as he was shaving in front of a window. Fortuitously for me, this particular policeman was involved in an organisation, 'The Escape', which operated in the south-east of Holland and had been responsible for the escape of quite a number of Allied aircrew. What I also did not know until many years later was that Herman was extremely reluctant to come to this particular airman's assistance since I was being harboured by a woman who was the most notorious gossip for miles around, both sides of the border. He therefore feared for his security if he stepped in.

Back in the cottage by dint of crude sign language we had got around to the subject of food which was beginning to get my attention as it was now Tuesday morning and I had eaten nothing since the bacon and egg in the mess before take-off on Saturday evening. Following agreement with my hosts that I was hungry I received two thick slices of black bread spread liberally with strong garlic dripping. I took a bite and chewed and, although in the next few months I was to get used to black bread, it was at this stage a completely new experience, particularly the garlic. My stomach almost revolted but not knowing what the food situation was it seemed a good idea to get used to it.

A little while later Herman Ankoné entered the house having apparently overcome his reservations about assisting me. At this stage I was unaware of his profession or nationality and, as he entered the room in civilian clothes barking out a command in German, I began to fear that, perhaps, I had been betrayed. However, after further attempts to test my understanding of German, we again resorted to sign language as Herman spoke only Dutch and German. Pen and paper were also forthcoming in an attempt to establish to everyone's satisfaction that I was an RAF officer who had landed the night before. It did not seem to do much for their confidence in me when I denied coming from the Lancaster the night before but had dropped in three nights previously. Eventually, appearing to be satisfied, Herman took his leave, having placed me alone in the sitting room to await a further caller who would visit me at 9:00 a.m. I sat there feeling rather isolated and wondering whether to take my leave, but at least my battledress was beginning to dry out as I tried to occupy myself with the effort of attempting to eat and keep down the black bread. Periodically one of the Belgians looked round the door to smile and reassure me.

Promptly at 9:00 a.m. the door opened and what proved to be a Dutch police officer entered the room. To say the least I was somewhat overawed by the dark green uniform worn by a very tall man heightened by a high pill-box type of cap. As he entered he took the same line as Herman, barking out commands in German but having no knowledge whatsoever of German I could only look at him in blank ignorance. There was probably also fear that perhaps I had after all come to the wrong house but then he switched to English in which he continued to interrogate me for a while to confirm my identity; the two or three Players cigarettes still left in my case helping to establish me. The officer proved to be Sergeant

YEAR 1944		AIRCRAFT			DUTY	TIME IN AIR			
						OBSERVER		GUNNER	
Month	Date	Type	No.	Pilot	(INCLUDING RESULTS AND REMARKS)	Day	Night	Day	Night
					C/F	310.45	203.30		
PRIL	6	HALIFAX III	'B' LK747	S/LDR SOMERSCALES	B/A AIR TEST	.50			
PRIL	16	HALIFAX III	'B' LK747	S/LDR SOMERSCALES	B/A X COUNTRY (WARLOAD)	5.30			
PRIL	17	HALIFAX III	'B' LK747	S/LDR SOMERSCALES	B/A AIR TEST	.30			
PRIL	18	HALIFAX III	"B" LK747	S/LDR SOMERSCALES	B/A OPS TERGNIER MARSHALLING YARDS 6×1000 LB HC 3×500 LB MC 6×500 DELAYS		4.45		
RIL	20	HALIFAX III	"B"	"	B/A AIR TEST	.25			
RIL	20	HALIFAX III	"B"	"	B/A OPS: OTTIGNIES 8×1000 LBS 7×500 LBS.		4.05		
IL	22	HALIFAX I	"I" M2578	"	B/A AIR TEST.	1.10			
RIL	22	HALIFAX III	"I"	"	OPS: DUSSELDORF. MISSING. A/C caught fire in Swing. 5 mins before target. Baled out. Pilot & MU. AG Killed. ENG. WOP + R.AG. P.O.W's NAV. RETURNED WITH SELF, HOME				
				*	Signed R. Buckst. S/L "O/C" "A" FLIGHT				
					Summary for April ——————→	8.25	8.45		
					TOTAL FLYING TIME	319.10	212.15		

Top left: Flight Lieutenant S. T. Wingham.
Top right: Squadron Leader S. Somerscales, DFC.
Bottom left: Wireless Officer F. J. Rowe.
Bottom right: Flying Officer J. H. Reavill, DFM.

Top left: Pilot Officer S. W. Stephen.
Top right: Jim and Nell Lewis, 1942.

Bottom: Reunion 1994, Herefordshire. Left to right:
Jim Lewis, Tom Wingham, Jack Reavill, Sid Stephen.

Top: No. 7 Air Observers' Course, 42 Air School, Port Elizabeth, South Africa in May 1942. 'Stu' Sloan stands in the second row, third from left. Tom Wingham is sitting in the front row, third from right. Frank Whittaker is in the second row, fifth from left.

Bottom: 1st Tour crew – 102 Squadron Pocklington, May 1943. Left to right standing: Joe Holliday (flight engineer), Dave Hewlett (pilot), 'Blackie' Blackallar (navigator), 'Chiefie' Beale (wireless operator). Left to right kneeling: Andy Reilly (air gunner), Tom Wingham (bomb aimer), Jim Nightingale (wireless operator – replacing Chiefie), Willie Hall (air gunner).

Top: Intensive Flying Development Flight, Boscombe Down, October 1943. First Production Halifax III. Air and groundcrews from 102 and 77 Squadrons. Author second from left kneeling.

Bottom left and right: First point of contact – Teuven 1944 and revisited in 1977.

Top left: Former police station, Slenaken. Extensively altered since 1944 for civil housing.

Top right: The Linckens' farmhouse.

Bottom: Ciska Linckens and the author in York circa 1984.

Opposite page, top: Left to right: Herman Ankoné, Tom Wingham, Richard and Ciska Linckens at a reunion in January 1977.

Opposite page, bottom: Madame Coomans, Tom Wingham and Mady. Bury St Edmunds, 1981.

Nº 08808

PRÉFECTURE DU NORD

CARTE D'IDENTITE

Nom : DENIS
Prénoms : Thomas.

Né le 20 janvier 1923
à Nancy
Département de Meurthe et Moselle.
Domicile : rue de
la Poste, 28 - Lille

SIGNALEMENT

Taille : 1m 70   Nez : allongé
Cheveux : châtain-clair. Forme Générale du
Moustache : néant   visage : ovale
Yeux : bleus-verts   Teint : pâle
Signes particuliers : néant.

Empreinte digitale,

Signature du Titulaire

A LILLE le 5 - 2 1942.

Pour le Préfet du Nord,
Le Chef de Division délégué,

Renouvellement.

Numéro 16376

Nom DENIS.

Prénoms Thomas Joseph.

État civil Célibataire.

Nationalité Belge
né à Nadrin (Pr. Lux.)
le 10 janvier 1923.

Profession Employé.

Résidence précédente Néant.

Seconde résidence Néant

Inscrit Vol. 4 Fol. 996

Rue Piedboeuf. nº 18

le 3 février 1943

Caisse de Retraite - Nº du Compte
(Loi du 10-12-1924)

Signature du porteur

Taille UN mètre cent.

Jupille, le 3 février 1943.
'Officier de l'État Civil (ou son délégué)

Quiconque falsifie la présente carte s'expose à une peine correctionnelle.

Vol. fol.	Date	Div.	Nº

Demeures successives à

RUE

(Voir suite au verso)

S. A. des Charbonnages
Steinkohlenbergbau A. G.

S⁺ A⁺⁺ DES CHARBONNAGES ⁺E
B⁺ ESPÉRANCE, BATTERIE & VIOLETTE
SIÈGE DE WANDRE à WANDRE

1944

CERTIFICAT
AUSWEIS

M **DENIS Thomas Joseph**
Hr
(nom, prénom)
(Name, Vorname)

né le **10 janvier 1923** à **Nandrin**
geboren am zu

demeurant à **Jupille** , rue **Piedboeuf** N° **18**
wohnhaft zu Strasse Nr

carte d'identité n° **16376** de **Jupille** (commune)
Personalausweis Nr von (Gemeinde)

est membre du Personnel de notre entreprise et y est occupé de **22** heures à **6** heures;
ist Mitglied der Belegschaft unseres Unternehmens und beschäftigt von Uhr bis Uhr;

éventuellement, de heures à heures.
beziehungsweise von Uhr bis Uhr.

Le **19 janvier** 1944.
Den 1944.

S⁺ A⁺⁺ DES CHARBONNAGES ⁺E
B⁺ ESPÉRANCE, BATTERIE & VIOLETTE
SIÈGE DE WANDRE à WANDRE
(cachet de la Société et signature
du représentant responsable)

N. B. — Le présent certificat ne peut être utilisé que pour les besoins du travail; il doit être restitué par le détenteur lorsque celui-ci cesse de faire partie du personnel.
N. B. — Der gegenwärtige Ausweis darf blos zu Arbeitszwecken benutzt werden; sein Inhaber hat denselben sofort zurück zu erstatten wenn er aufhört Mitglied der Belegschaft zu sein.
396-15 101

Opposite page, top: French ID card.
Opposite page, bottom: Belgian ID card.

Top: Work certificate providing evidence of a job on the night shift at the local coal mines of Wandré.
Bottom: Marie Warnant, 1945.

1896 - 1971

1902 - 1996

Opposite page, top: The Schoofs family. Left to right: M. Schoofs, Jenny, Andrée, Mme. Schoofs and Pascal.

Opposite page, bottom: M. and Mme. Schoofs.

Top: Pascal, Andrée, Tom Wingham and Jenny in 2005.

Bottom: Jim Lewis (centre) with two other evaders and their helper. In a house near Liège Cathedral, September 1944.

Top left: Chateau Sinnich, home of the Count de Secillon who aided Jim Lewis's escape.

Top right: Farmhouse at Lockerplei (circa 1988), Sid Stephen's first port of call after the crash.

Bottom left: First Communion dress made from Sid's parachute for Maria Boers by her mother.

Bottom right: The remains of Stephen's parachute, Lockerplei. Left to right: Leonie Boormans (Ciska's daughter), Tom Wingham, Ciska Linckens and Leo Pierey.

Top: Site of crash. The port wing was found in the woods to the left, one engine in the clearing and the fuselage and starboard wing in Wagelerbos to the right.

Bottom left: Jim Lewis's flying helmet. Recovered in Mechelen, circa 1988. It now resides in the Yorkshire Air Museum.

Bottom right: Piece of armour plate from behind the pilot's seat. Lockerplei circa 1989.

Top left: Dutch farmer with propeller blade of MZ578.

Top right: Tom Wingham revisiting the crash site in 1988.

Bottom: Jack Reavill returns to Wagelerbos in 1994.

Top: Memorial to Stan Somerscales and Harry Poole on the edge of Wagelerbos.

Bottom: Tom Wingham, RAF Liaison Officer and Jack Reavill 1994.

Top left and right: Maastricht Cemetery.

Bottom: Reunion of former RAF Escaping Society members, Brussels, October 2008. Left to right: Ray Worrall, Bob Frost, Bob Barclay, Freddie, Gordon Mellor, Tom Wingham, John Berthelsen.

Vermeulen of the Dutch local police stationed at the village of Slenaken just the other side of the border from Teuven. He had brought some clothes with him so that I was now able to change my uniform for black coat and pin-stripe trousers, Vermeulen taking the uniform for disposal. He also requested my silk maps and photographs, the maps presumably because they were a give-away if caught with them and the photographs (three passport size) which aircrew carried in order to facilitate the forgery of papers for their escape. These formalities having been completed it was now time to move and having ensured the coast was clear we crossed the road, went round the back of the house opposite, where, with many apologies, I was shown an outdoor toilet in which I was to hole up for the day. The sergeant would come back with others at about 6:00 in the evening to collect me.

Anyone who has spent eight hours in a toilet will appreciate that time does tend to drag. The toilet was the wood bench type on which I sat to one side. Being isolated and confined in a space three foot by four in a strange land, with only a half eaten slice of black bread with garlic dripping for company, gave plenty of time for thought. Had I done the right thing to put myself in other people's hands or should I, now that I was out of uniform, take a chance and have a go on my own? Still suffering from concussion meant that my whole body had to be rotated towards whatever had to be viewed and any slight turn of my head caused immediate blurring of vision, so, on balance, it seemed best to have faith in my present friends. After the previous night's storm the sky was now clear and the warm sun shining on my cramped quarters made it necessary to get some ventilation by opening the door slightly which, as it faced on to fields, did not cause any problem. And so the day wore on.

Between 5:00 and 6:00 p.m. Sergeant Vermeulen re-appeared and said that we were going back to Holland in company with two other Dutch policemen, one of whom was Herman Ankoné, now in uniform, who would precede us to make sure that the road was clear. Emerging from the rear of the house my escort waited to receive a signal from Herman at the end of the village street before we set off after him along the secondary Teuven-Slenaken road, maintaining a distance of about one hundred yards from the two officers ahead. After a mile or so we reached a farm where, being met by the farmer, I was quickly led into a barn and lifted up into the hay loft with instructions to stay there till nightfall. With the dark came my police escorts again, so, leaving the remains of the garlic-coated black bread in the hay loft, I accompanied them for a short walk to a Dutch farmhouse where I was welcomed by Richard and Ciska Linckens. My hosts were but five years older than me, Richard being somewhat thin and wiry standing about five feet seven inches tall, while Ciska, his wife, was a plumpish and stolid Dutch woman about an inch shorter. The front door opened into a hall which divided the house in two and I was led into the room on the right which proved to be the dining room where I was sat down, preparatory to being given a meal. The police departed as Ciska brought some food to the table. Eating alone in Ciska's company I discovered that she had a daughter of just over one year old and was expecting a further child in about four weeks time. She nursed the baby on her lap as I ate, but she suddenly tensed and, with her fingers to her lips, enjoined silence. There were voices outside and doors opening and shutting as visitors joined Richard for coffee in the sitting room on the other side of the hallway. They were the German border guards cultivated by Richard to give him some sort of cover in his activities in helping Allied aircrew.

In recording these events nearly fifty years on one still remembers the incredible bravery of those people throughout Europe who organised and gave shelter to aircrew. The penalty for helping aircrew was quite specific; execution for men and consignment to a concentration camp for women. Even now, I remember my fear for the safety of this unemotional and pragmatic Dutch woman and her child put at risk by my presence in her house. At the time I was in ignorance of being the thirty-ninth airman who had been helped on his way by Richard and Ciska across the border to a Belgian escape line; Richard's role being to distract the German guards by visiting them at their post or otherwise engaging them while his wife signalled by displaying a sheet from an upstairs' window when all was clear. I was the last of that thirty-nine and, indeed, the only one whose name they knew and who slept over in the farmhouse. Richard died in May 1977 but the visit I made shortly before his death assisted in the posthumous award of the Dutch Resistance Cross in 1984 which is highly prized by his widow. When the Germans had left, I was taken upstairs to a bedroom and after a wash, with great relief, was able to fall upon the bed and make up for the four lost days of sleep. Apart from that, very little remains with me of the time spent in that farm at Heijenrade.

After a further night when the border guards again interrupted my evening meal to take coffee with Richard, the decision was taken to move me on. Late the following evening, the three police officers collected their charge and we moved off towards Slenaken in the same formation as before. It was not far, probably about one and a half miles but, about half way there, as we descended a hill, there were voices and laughter ahead. Vermeulen grabbed my arm and whispered, "German guards!" We waited until we heard the Dutch officers saying goodnight and the Germans moved up the hill before Vermeulen whispered to me to hide in the orchard by the side of the road. I ducked through the wire fence and Vermeulen strode off towards the advancing Germans to pass the time of night. When the road was clear he returned back with the others to collect me and resume our journey to the village. In Slenaken there were three houses which served as the police station and housing for the local officers, one of which was occupied by Sergeant Vermeulen with his wife and two young children, both under five years. Again, I could not but worry for the safety of the family upon whose life I was intruding which was heightened by the sense of fear around me that I could feel until I left Holland. Many years later I was told about the woman at Teuven whom I had initially contacted whose reliability of keeping her mouth shut was in much doubt. It was such cases that provoked that sense of fear.

The following day Vermeulen, when he returned after work to the house, told me what happened to my crew. Stan Somerscales and Harry Poole had been killed, Sid Stephen, John Rowe and Jack Reavill were all in hospital as POWs, and there was one unidentified body. It was unbelievable. Six days ago we were all together in York drinking the evening away. We were fireproof, all having completed a tour of ops and a period as instructors before coming together for a second tour. Now this news! The unidentified body could only be Jim Lewis who I had helped on his way through the escape hatch; but if so, why had he died? And the rest of the crew – what had happened to produce such casualties, for there had seemed to be plenty of time for them to get out. It was to be forty-eight years before I comprehended the full horror of what happened to those six friends with whom I flew.

*   *   *

Hank Iveson, the CO of 76 Squadron, told me that he always had a conscience about the loss of Stan Somerscales after he was taken off the Dortmund raid. Hank's son was shot down over the Falklands and subsequently evaded capture by the Argentineans to regain the British lines. In 1983 after a 4 Group reunion in York, Hank shared a cab with me and following a short discussion it seemed apt to quote to him the old biblical saying, "the sins of the father shall be visited on the children." He laughed, but confessed that he had always suffered from a guilty conscience at the loss of flight commanders he had selected for the squadron from the HCU at Rufforth.

*   *   *

After contact with Leo Pierey in 1989, it seemed to be time to resolve the queries I had about the crash so many years before, so I set about finding the surviving crew members to record their accounts. It was easy to find Jack Reavill, he was still living at his old address in Nottingham carrying on the family business, but it was more difficult with John Rowe and Sid Stephen. I eventually traced John, who had gone back to his old county of Cornwall, and Sid, who had emigrated to Australia. From them I was able to piece together the whole story.

Almost immediately upon the order to bale out, John Rowe, in the rear turret, had already run into trouble and his situation soon became desperate. His seat had been in the fully depressed position to give him as much downward vision over the guns as possible but now the seat refused to return to its normal position, probably due to damaged hydraulics. This meant that his legs were jammed under the guns making it almost impossible to leave the turret. He rotated it manually to the 'fore and aft' position then slid open the turret doors before reaching behind to get the bulkhead doors open. Everything in the dark had to be done by touch and with his hands behind his back. In John's own words:

> "I found my chute in the rack and pulled it into the turret over my head. I was dead scared I was going to catch the rip handle in something and open the chute prematurely; I clipped it on and manually turned the turret on the beam. The seat was still stuck so it made it pretty difficult to get through the turret doors and, with the aircraft belting down in a port spin, I was being thrown all over the place. Eventually, I was left in the position of hanging outside by my knees over the turret ring, with my feet trapped under the guns because of the seat, being spun around by the doomed aircraft. I got one leg out and then eventually wriggled my other leg out of the boot leaving it in the turret. Falling clear I pulled the cord and all was well when all the noise, smoke and flames suddenly stopped."

Pilot Officer Sid Stephen was in his normal position as flight engineer, directly behind the pilot, when the Halifax was hit by a nightfighter with 'schräge musik' cannon, piloted by Oberfeldwebel Rudolf Frank. The Halifax was the Oberfeldwebel's forty-third kill, but he too was nearing the end of his career. On the night of 26th April, after having shot down a further two RAF bombers, he also was shot down near Eindhoven, and killed with his crew, whether by a Lancaster or a 'Serrate' (radar detecting) Mosquito is not certain. He was posthumously promoted to Leutnant. Of this Sid was not to know anything for another forty-eight years. But then schräge-musik seems to have been a secret kept just as well by the Air Ministry in late 1943 and early 1944 as it was by the Germans. Certainly very few operational aircrew were made aware of this type of attack.

When Stan gave the order to bale out Sid put on his parachute and then checked to see whether it was possible to halt the fire. The extinguishers were inadequate and seeing the wing was on fire by the bomb bays he realized the fire was beyond control and came back to the cockpit with the intention of going out of the forward escape hatch which he could see being opened by Jim and myself. However, as Jack Reavill, who was getting Stan's parachute, stood blocking his way forward Stan ordered him to go out through the rear door. Sid turned back into the smoke-filled fuselage only to meet Harry Poole, the mid-upper gunner, who was coming forward. Being without intercom, Sid grabbed Harry by the arm, turned him round and they made their way back to the rear hatch. But the hatch wouldn't open, which is probably why Harry was coming forward. It seemed to take an age working on the catches, with both of them crouching in the dark with Sid levering his feet against the hatch before, in Sid's words, "we eventually opened the hatch and that's the last I remember before awakening in the air just above the edge of a wood which had been set on fire by our aircraft!" It is probable that a wing had dropped off at the same time as they had got the door open thus throwing Syd through the hatch as the aircraft went into the spin which was throwing John all over the sky in the rear turret. Four had now reached the ground and there was to be only one more survivor, Jack Reavill.

Upon receiving the order to bale out Jack keyed a distress call to base on the radio and then clipped on his own parachute as he made his way up to the cockpit. Locating the pilot's chute, he unstowed it and then reached across trying to assist Stan to clip on his harness. Suddenly, there was an explosion, the aircraft went into a spin and Jack was in the grip of G forces which rendered him helpless. There must have been another explosion throwing him clear, of which he knew nothing, for he woke up to find himself free falling with no parachute on his chest. As he came to and sized up his predicament he realised that his parachute was still with him, floating above his head, attached to one strap of his harness. Reaching out he managed to release the parachute. Barely had it cracked open to check his fall than he hit a tree and then the ground.

In the official Dutch local archives the following is recorded.

> About one o'clock in the night from 22 to 23 April 1944 a twin-engined English aircraft, type Halifax, exploded in the air and came down in pieces. The fragments lie scattered in Mechelen wood, in an adjoining meadow, and in Wachelder wood right opposite in the municipality of Gulpen. The fuselage and the right wing are situated upside down in Wachelder wood, the tail, two engines and a part of the fuselage in the meadow and the left wing and other fragments in Mechelen wood.
>
> About nine o'clock in the morning -------- I myself arrived at the spot -----. Then I charged myself with blocking off the ground and searching the woods and I found two dead men; one dead in the fuselage of the aircraft ----.
>
> On April 23 the two dead have been transferred to the Saint Joseph home at Gulpen and on April 24 they have been taken by the Manager of the General Cemetery at Maastricht.
>
> Truthfully drawn up by me on 24 April 1944.
>
> The Commander of the APPS Gulpen A.H.A. HEIDENDAL.

The official German communiqué stated that Squadron leader S. Somerscales, Flight Sergeant H. Poole and one unidentified airman were killed and Pilot Officer W. Stephen, Flying Officer J. Reavill and Acting Warrant Officer J. Rowe were prisoners of war. This information was at a later date passed to the International Red Cross at Geneva. No satisfactory explanation has ever been discovered for the 'unidentified body' given out by the Germans. One can only speculate that perhaps the local German commander was seeking to discourage the local Resistance from helping two evaders or was covering his own back against charges of allowing two aircrew to escape rather than just one. There now seems to be no likelihood of a satisfactory answer.

At the time I made the immediate assumption that the unidentified body had to be Jim Lewis, although how and why he should be dead baffled me since I had seen him safely out of the aircraft. Later, from what I remembered of our chats together and with the assistance of others, I managed to draw up the following account of Jim's evasion and return to the UK.

Chapter VII

The Firquet Escape Line

Jim Lewis was the first out of the aircraft with my assistance. He had squeezed through the dark hole and, after a push, dropped away into the darkness, only to find that the slipstream had whipped away one of his boots as he emerged from the Halifax. His parachute having opened, he drifted downwards, watching the blazing aircraft explode and later crash into the ground. In a short time, Jim too had landed but, in the black of the night had been unable to avoid crashing into some trees on the edge of a wood and, with his parachute caught up in the trees, was still a number of feet from the ground.

In the dark it took Jim some time to disentangle his harness and parachute from the trees and safely descend to the ground without further damage. Crashing into the trees had given him a cracked rib and injury to his shoulder; while losing that boot had not helped when his foot hit the branches of a tree. He sat down and started to rip off pieces of the parachute to wrap around his foot in order to enable him to walk cross-country to seek help. Having done this, he hid the harness and parachute as best he could before moving off.

Unfortunately, about four years before compiling this account Jim Lewis had suffered a stroke and lost his power of speech, and with it, the ability to write. As a result, it was necessary to look elsewhere for information on his evasion. This can always be a difficult task as, even now, there are often people prepared to make up all sorts of stories about their activities during the war which are often very plausible but complete fabrication. The following is one such story related by Jeu Van Mersch.

On the night of the crash Jeu Van Mersch had gone to bed early. He was the thirty-year-old son of the farmer at the great farm of Hommerich and was due to rise early to carry out the milking. During the night something had woken him but getting up, looking out of the window and seeing nothing, he returned to bed and slept till 5:00 a.m. when he dressed and took himself off to the cowsheds. About an hour later as he carried out the milking he was disturbed by Jim who had found his way to the farm in the early morning light. Jeu knew no English and not too much French while Jim Lewis had not one word of Dutch but did have some French from his schooldays. Communication was difficult and laborious, taking a long time for understanding to be reached. Jim eventually made Jeu realise that his aircraft had crashed in the woods across the fields and that he had heard a cry for help coming from the vicinity. Hiding Jim in the big barn by the house Jeu saddled his horse and rode out to search for the injured airman. From Hommerich he rode south-west and initially saw nothing. The only sound was the rustle of the wind through the trees which were lit by the rising sun and, as the dawn chorus of the birds began to reach its peak, everything looked so peaceful. As Jeu moved in the direction given by Jim a human cry interrupted the stillness. On the edge of Mechelen wood he tied his horse to a tree and walked across the meadow where he found Jack Reavill lying severely injured a few yards into the Wageler wood. About fifty yards further into the wood the Halifax fuselage was lying upside down with a dead airman inside. There was nothing Jeu could do on his own so, covering the wounded airman with his coat and after indicating that he was going for help, Jeu went back to collect his horse and ride down to Mechelen, the nearest village to the crash, in order to get Dr Janssen for Jack.

Later that morning Jeu returned to the farm where he had Jim in hiding and began to face up to his problem. All his family, father, brothers and uncles were well-known for their pro-German sympathies so he was unable to confide in his family about the man in the barn. He started to sneak food from the table but liquids were more difficult and when his mother questioned what he was doing he had to take her into his confidence. Fortunately, being a mother, she gave him assistance, but, nevertheless, was unable to help him solve the major problem, namely, how to move Jim on to a safer haven. As soon as he tried to discuss the matter with people who he suspected had the necessary contacts he ran into a wall of silence because of the family connections and the fear of a German trap.

Eventually Jeu went to Vaals to consult with Mr Noppeney, known as almost certainly a member of the resistance movement, who made it quite plain that no one in the area was likely to get involved with him because of his family's sympathies and that the only course of action would be for Jeu to take Jim south over the Belgian border and tell him to seek help there. This was the only advice Jeu could get and so, having hidden Jim for, he said, four weeks he now took him down to Geiven in Belgium and left him near the station. Unfortunately, because of the language barrier Jim was under the impression that he would be picked up there by a member of the Resistance and it took some time before he realised he had been abandoned.

This fanciful story is completely at odds with Jim Lewis's recollections which are contained in a letter written a number of years ago which was published in the memoirs of a member of the Dutch Resistance. The relevant passage from the letter reads:

> "I landed (heavily) in forest country and thought I might be in Germany. I walked west all night, hid in a wood next day and walked again the second night. At dawn I came to a shrine with a Dutch inscription so knew I was in Holland. I met then a young man who recognised my uniform. He took me to a farm nearby, an elderly couple gave me food, hid me in a barn and promised help. I cannot remember names – I was pretty shocked and had a broken rib. It was about 1km from the Belgian border. I was given civilian clothes, left my uniform at the farm, and was

escorted by a man on foot into Belgium on 24 April. I was
alone".

In the light of the above it is not possible to accept Jeu's story at face
value and yet, Jim had lost a boot and Jeu mentioned this. He also
stated that he had left Jim alone in Belgium. How he came by this
knowledge, it is difficult to say, but there is no doubt that Jim was
never in the Hommerich barn.

Jim's precise movements for the next week or so are uncertain but
it is probable that he stayed with a Belgian farmer for a day or two
before being taken to the Chateau Sinnich, the family home of the
Count de Secillon. Quite a few airmen on their way down from
Holland stayed under the shelter of the count who had spent some
time being tortured by the Gestapo, who, suspecting his activities,
but unable to prove them, left their mark on his body which was
scarred badly with lash marks.

How long Jim stayed at the chateau is not known but he had most
certainly left there by the second week in May for, during the last
two weeks, in company with other RAF, Canadian and American
evaders he took part in a journey south aimed at reaching
Switzerland. Early in May, when I was in Wandré, I had been asked
whether I wished to make the journey to Switzerland but had turned
downed the offer as I wished to regain England and not be interned
for the rest of the war. This was probably the journey I turned down.

Jim was one of perhaps twenty aircrew of various nationalities
who had been assembled and sheltered in a former monastery of the
Holy Cross church near the centre of Liège, preparatory to being
sent on their way back home. They were under the wing of a
resistance movement known as the Group Firquet who, whatever
their past history, in this case went well down the road to producing
a near disaster. An account of the journey in which Jim Lewis took
part follows. Written by Frank Caubergh a young member of the
Group Firquet it could almost be used as the basis for farce by a TV
script writer. The following article, then, is actually as written by him

some forty years after the events described.

A Memorable Day in May 1944
By F. Caubergh (Belgian Resistance)

During World War II, while Belgium was under German occupation, I became a member of an underground resistance movement known as Group Firquet, which specialized in the hiding and repatriation of Allied airmen who had been shot down, mostly over Belgium or Holland, but some over Germany. Our group had its headquarters in the cloisters of the Holy Cross church, almost in the centre of Liège. These cloisters had been for centuries occupied by monks, but now, and for many years, by ordinary families, access to these small dwellings being directly through the church or by an independent entry further along the street, but still near to the church. Hundreds of American, Canadian, Australian and British airmen have crossed this church (probably without any thought of crossing themselves), to stay for some time in this modest building, surrounded by a neat little garden, to await false identity and working papers, new clothes and a place to be lodged and fed until the opportunity arose for the final trip into France and Switzerland.

For many months, despite the fact that I had been obliged to perform compulsory work in a German factory and had been investigated by the Gestapo, I had taken every chance to assist the group, principally by finding hiding places for the evaders, getting coupons, money and supplies whenever and wherever they could be obtained and, even on occasion acting as interpreter, having learnt English at an evening school, until the commandant decided that I would be more use in Germany. When I speak of finding food, hiding places, etc., one should not forget that in 1944 the Allied bombing of Germany had intensified; more airmen were being attracted to the Tower of the Holy Cross (L'Eglise Sainte Croix), just as ship-wrecked sailors are to a lighthouse. Then, one day, what I was hoping for happened. I was informed that I was to accompany a bunch of airmen to France and the Swiss border; and, receiving some French money and false identity papers, made ready for this new venture.

The next day, a nice spring morning in May, was to be a day that I will never forget, even though some facts and faces may have dimmed somewhat. It is also a day when we took many chances, but yet, were not made to pay for the big faults which we committed, and which might have had disastrous consequences. First; we all had our photograph taken together (this is still in existence) just as for a wedding group. Not only the men who were to leave, but also those who were resident in the house at that time, how stupid !!!! Next, the truck. This was just a small vehicle, not at all suitable for transporting people, so that day, early in the morning came the hammering and nailing of benches, so as to enable at least twenty people to be seated for what was to be a long journey. A big red cross was painted on the roof and we all received a badge supposed to disguise us as Red Cross workers. I bet we would not have resisted two minutes of interrogation in the event of capture! Once these preparations finished we all boarded the vehicle, the local Parish priest threw some Holy Water on it, blessed us and wished us all a safe journey.

Off we went; thirteen allied airmen, four Belgian escorts, and the driver. Perhaps here I should mention a few names, at least those that I remember: Donald Brinkhurst, Jim Lewis, Jim Goebel, Peter Holmes, Robert Tucker, Charlie Westerland, Phil Solomon, Georges Flather and Pavelka. I see no reason to name the Belgian escorts, as I think that in the meantime they have all died, and even if they proved to be courageous men at other times, in this instance, I believe, they all failed.

We left in the late morning, crossing the town in the direction of the Ardennes. I cannot remember the exact route but think that it was in the direction of Dinant, Philippeville and I know for certain that we crossed Florennes because our guardian angel must have been with us at this stage. We must have passed directly across a German airfield, for I saw distinctly camouflaged German aircraft, probably Messerschmitts, alongside the road which was very wide at this point and used by the Germans for take-offs and landings, the area being heavily guarded by German sentries. At one point, a car preceding our truck was ordered to stop and a German signalled to our driver also to halt. Our driver ignored this order and drove on and, through a hole in the tarpaulin, I clearly saw the soldier lift his rifle to his shoulder ready to fire. For whatever reason he did not!! Why? Because he changed his mind? Because he saw the red cross? Or was it simply that we were meant to be lucky that day? Had he fired there would have been a massacre, or at least a fine capture which would, no doubt, have procured for him a Cross of Merit. Apart from this incident, which could have been disastrous, the trip proved uneventful.

We reached Bois de Bruly where we all alighted and quickly disappeared into the woods, seventeen men walking in pairs, and I remember being in the middle of the column paired with Charlie Westerland. After hours of walking and hiding, occasionally without shelter, we arrived at the small village of Bruly, to be met by the customs officer and his wife who had been informed of our impending arrival.

The airmen were lodged in the upstairs room of a café

near the main road; I was taken to a small castle nearby, occupied at the time by a fine family from Ostend and who, at the time were hiding a lot of Jewish children. The other three Belgians stayed at the café and at the customs officer's house. In the evening after supper and with twilight drawing on, the lady of the castle wanted to say "Hello" to the aircrew boys; so with some other members of the family we went down to the village centre. As we neared the café the sound of raised voices and cries were heard and, on opening the door, a pitched battle could be seen in progress between a bunch of obviously drunken men and an hysterical woman who was not the least violent of the crowd. I tried to intervene and calm them down to draw their attention to their responsibilities and to the danger that this disturbance could bring to all of us. But I was furiously told to "shut up" as they were the bosses and I was merely a greenhorn to the job. The noise had gone on for some time and could be clearly heard outside with the main road not too far away and German convoys passing by regularly. The irresponsibility of these men on whom one was supposed to rely was really astonishing and, perhaps, explains why they later died by their own carelessness. Finally, as darkness came and the drunken men had fallen asleep we got the airmen out of their rooms with the aid of the people at the castle and, under cover of darkness, took them along the railway to the castle, where each was provided with a blanket, from where we walked to a convent at Petit-Chappelle.

The only inhabitants of the convent at that time were an old monk and his sister. They were Flemish, which at once made the contact between them and myself easier, as I too am Flemish. Next morning I faced three very ashamed men who had had the thirteen airmen, for whom they had been responsible, 'kidnapped' from under their very noses. But also that night, due to intense bombing, the escape chain, which had been long established, had been broken; so the decision was taken that to proceed further would be useless and dangerous. The two eldest of the four-man escort would return to Liège, find the truck, and take us all back there. These two left immediately, leaving behind myself and the other guy along with fourteen airmen, the fourteenth being an American who had been shot down the day before and had joined up with our party. After two days my companion was of the opinion that our comrades were taking a long time in returning for us and he also left in order to find out the reason for the delay, leaving me alone with the party of fourteen airmen.

Each day I went, basket on arm, to the village to do the shopping and find whatever fruit and food that was available at the time. Naturally, the villages and peasant country were better provided for than the towns and quite a lot could be obtained, if one had money. I must say, our stay at the convent was not disagreeable, the place was nice and clean, we had a large dormitory for our group alone, the beds were comfortable, and the monk's sister did the cooking for us. Also, we had at our disposal a large playground, which was excellent for exercise, to keep us in good shape for what may lay ahead: and last, but not least, we played interminable card games. The main road was not too far away and, more than once, I had to ask for less buoyancy, chiefly from the Americans who did not seem conscious of the existing danger, but they were so young and full of life! They do say, "The nicest song does not last long", and that was to be so with our holiday in war-time.

The priest, who was obviously uncomfortable at our long stay and feared for the lives of his sister and himself, asked me if we could leave as soon as possible, due to the fact that the following day some clergymen would be arriving for a religious retreat. He said that he could not run the risk of these people seeing us as he was ignorant of their political views, and that it was a fact that in Belgium, both before and during the war, some of the clergy had mani-fested sympathy for the socialist-democrat views of the German regime. It would be a lie to say that I was happy with this announcement, but there was nothing for it but to seek another place to shelter, and this I started to do immediately. I was lucky; I found an old deserted house that had once been a parochial patronage, where youths met and played theatre, now partly destroyed and full of rubbish, but it had to do! It was not far from the convent and that night each of us, with a blanket and some food, crossed the street under cover of darkness and sneaked into our new palace. At that time of year, the end of May, the nights were still cold and we passed many shivering hours, all except that shrewd man Donald Brinkhurst who had quickly found some old theatre-cloth in which to wrap himself. Next morning we were awakened, at least those of us who had managed to sleep, by the cries of children who were peering through the broken windows at this bunch of strange men. This meant, of course, that we could no longer remain there, but this time, being alone with fourteen men in an unknown place, and with our only resource being the people at the castle, I had to look for help.

At the castle I found a small truck and, by threes and fours, all the airmen were taken to a remote farm in the middle of the woods. Here, the Americans were not long in finding an old radio and we were then entertained to an exhibition of how a boogie-woogie could be danced. This musical interlude, however, did not make us forget that our situation remained precarious. I started once more, this time on a bike, for my daily shopping in the village but did not have to do this many more times, as soon after our escape to the woods, the truck from Liège finally arrived to pick us up for our return there. The plan to return us all counted without the opinion of Donald Brinkhurst, once mid-upper gunner in a Lancaster bomber shot down over Germany, who succeeded in dodging German patrols and crossing borders and after much suffering and hiding reached our group in Liège. Here, as I remember, he was never really in hiding, but went naturally out walking, despite the Germans' presence, and, I have been told, even went swimming in the city's swimming pool whilst they were there. Now he had a goal – Switzerland; and did not agree one bit with our plan to go backward instead of forward, and had even collected five or six followers. Once the decision was taken we all left together that old farm, deep in the forest, where we had been so happy to find a short-term refuge at a critical point in our journey. We left together, but our roads were soon to separate. Six or seven remained on the truck bound for Liège; Donald, with the other airmen, myself and another guide took the direction of Rocroi.

Up to now, to the best of my belief, I have given a true account of this period of my life forty years ago which I spent with fourteen young men, all of about my own age, who had once dropped from the skies whilst engaged in the fight against the German tyrant. I cannot remember what happened immediately afterwards. For instance, my memory is completely blank as to how and where we separated, where we said good-bye and good luck and shook hands. I remember taking a train some place which was stopped before entering Louvain because the town was being bombed and the station and hospital had been hit. I still see myself seated on an empty beer cask on a big brewery truck from Alken, near St. Troud, from where I

got on to a tram which took me back home to Liège after
a two week absence.

In conclusion, one could say that our escape – tentative,
had not been a success – but was it really a failure after all?
The men who returned to Liège were lodged at the
cathedral. Later on, I once spent an afternoon with them at
the guardian's house. Here they patiently awaited liberation by their comrades, who were not far off anymore.

So ends the account by Frank Caubergh which is relative to Jim
Lewis's experience and is agreed by Don Brinkhurst. The narrative
does contain a final paragraph about Donald Brinkhurst's journey to
Switzerland and finally the UK but this has been omitted since it is
not relevant to this story.

After returning to Liège, as recounted by Frank Caubergh, Jim
Lewis and the remaining aircrew members of the failed 'home run'
were lodged in the cathedral. The bishop was decorated by several
countries at the end of hostilities for his work throughout the war in
sheltering political refugees and evading aircrew. The cathedral had
a long history in this type of work much of which was carried out in
the First World War when Liège was previously under the control of
the Germans. Here Jim was to stay for the next three months.

There was apparently a long-established routine to which the
evaders had to conform. During the day they were confined to their
'quarters' in the roof and behind the organ loft, being able to read,
play cards and engage in other sedentary activities. In the early
evening, after the cathedral was closed and locked to visitors, the
guardian would signal them to come out, when they could exercise
in the church, take food and sometimes go into various houses
attached to the cathedral precincts. On one particular day there was
a hitch in the routine. Closing time had come and gone without any
signal that they were free to leave their hidey-holes. Thinking that
the guardian had overlooked them Jim was volunteered to go out to
reconnoitre, this decision being taken on the basis that Jim's French

had improved a little since his arrival and was better than anyone else's.

Out into the deserted church went our volunteer. All was quiet. Across to the main door just to check – it was still unlocked! Obviously, the guardian had been held up somewhere so Jim decided to carry out the task of bolting the doors but, to his consternation, as he went to do so, was confronted by a German officer seeking entry. Quickly weighing up the situation Jim realised that there was no retreat, he had to bluff it out. The German was accompanied by a Belgian girlfriend who was likely to recognize his accent, so he thought up what he was to say then rattled it off as fast as possible in his schoolboy French hoping that the girl would not give him away. The conversation became a dialogue between Jim and the German in which Jim pointed out that the cathedral was overdue to close and, in spite of the officer's protest that he had made a special journey for the visit, managed to persuade him to defer his entry until a more convenient time the next day. With great relief Jim watched the officer and his girlfriend turn away before thankfully shutting up shop for the night.

Early in September the American army liberated Liège enabling Jim to come out of hiding and get down to Paris on the way home to his wife and the baby born during his absence. In the lobby of the George V Hotel he saw a familiar figure collecting a key from the desk and then move towards the lift. It was a joyous reunion that night as Jim and I celebrated our successful evasion.

Chapter VIII

Behind Bars

Coming to, at the edge of the woods, Sid Stephen could see by the light of the flames from the burning aircraft on the other side of the wood that he had a great gash on the back of his leg and could feel that his forehead had also been cut with blood streaming down his face. For a while he was unable to move but, when he eventually tried, he found himself in agony and thought he had broken a leg. On further examination he concluded that he had only sustained a badly sprained ankle so gathered up his parachute and started to wander around looking for somewhere to hide the bundle when he bumped into a young Dutch farmer who had come out to view the crash. Sid did not know who was the most surprised, he or the farmer, who seeing that Sid was badly hurt helped him to shelter in the Lockerplei farm.

As he entered Sid must have been a pretty gruesome sight with big open wounds on his forehead, blood-matted hair, a big open gash in his left buttock, blood encrusted ripped trousers and, to crown it all, two lovely black eyes. There was some argument between the farmer and his wife about calling a doctor, but in due course they came to agreement and Heer Boers, the farmer, left and in time returned with a doctor. In the meantime his wife tried to clean up Sid's face and offered a cup of ersatz coffee, no milk or sugar, which tasted vile. A number of neighbours had in the meantime called at the house and when the doctor arrived he spoke to Sid in English and told him that had he got to him earlier he could have attended to his wounds without informing the Germans but now too many people knew of his arrival. He then departed to telephone the Dutch police.

It is difficult for Britons who have never had to live under an alien occupying force to understand the fears, suspicions and hates engendered by such conditions. Sadly this atmosphere often led to results which nobody wanted. The farmer tried to explain to Sid that if he had not been wounded he would have passed him to the escape line. In turn the policeman said the same thing and indeed the doctor is believed to have patched up several aircrew before helping them on their way. But in the end Sid was collected and taken by a young Dutch police officer to the police station at Gulpen which, being a rural district, was also his home. Here his wife, who spoke some English, cooked a couple of eggs supplied by the farmer but Sid had no appetite and, with great difficulty, persuaded the couple to eat them, but only after promising that he would not tell the Germans. They then made up a bed in one of the cells, but left the door unlocked, a pretty safe bet since he was in no condition to make off.

After six hours sleep, Sid was awoken with a cup of coffee and a slice of black bread both of which he found quite unpalatable; two German guards and a sergeant came to collect him, taking him in a gas-propelled bus to a school commandeered by the Luftwaffe. Here he met up with John Rowe. Whilst there, two other sergeants came to them for assistance in identifying the two dead bodies at the site of the crash. Sid, knowing Stan well over two years, was able to identify him by a pound note from his top pocket which he always carried, together with his whistle, and being told that the other was near to the rear escape hatch knew that this had to be Harry, since nobody else could have been in that position. After being given the usual 'Red Cross' form to fill in, ostensibly to advise relatives that they were safe, they completed the name, rank and number and left the rest blank. This form was always produced for a new POW and had a whole range of questions relating to the individual's family, as well as a sequence of questions on his squadron, its CO, aircraft flown and strength etc. The two of them were then taken to separate rooms for interrogation, which was quite short, and then after a considerable delay were collected by three German guards and a sergeant and journeyed to the main hospital at Maastricht.

The hospital was staffed by nuns who, with the doctors, only spoke in whispers as they shuffled silently around. Here they were washed and cleaned up and their injuries dealt with and one nun even set to on Sid's ripped trousers in an attempt to repair them. By this time he was feeling hungry but the black bread with some sort of meat which was provided made eating a "throat gagging chore". Following a short sojourn here another gas-propelled bus appeared with three guards and a sergeant to transport them to a hospital at Tegelen. On arrival, John and Sid were taken to a room on the fourth floor with a barred window, a guard in the room and a locked door with another guard outside. How they expected them to escape was something that Sid was never able to work out but it seemed to both of them to be a worthwhile effort since it appeared that the two of them were tying up about a dozen troops. The food was a little better, although the ersatz coffee remained almost undrinkable. With no reading matter and, obviously, no radio, time dragged. On two occasions Luftwaffe pilots visited them to try to find out how they had been shot down, but at that time they did not know.

After four or five days, Sid was taken to the operating theatre where a huge German orderly was sharpening a cut throat razor. He grabbed Sid by the forelock and, with one clean sweep, cut his hair from front to back and it was with great relief that Sid found he wasn't having his throat cut! It was certainly a scary moment. His stitches and clips were removed before being returned to the ward. About this time an Australian air gunner from 10 Squadron, a Sergeant Smith, was brought into the ward, completely encased in plaster. When shot down, he had been unable to rotate his turret and while going forward to the rear escape hatch wearing a complete Irvin flying suit he became caught between the fuselage and the rear wheel cover and was not able to extricate himself. He went down with the aircraft and, on impact, was thrown some 200 yards from the crash, as a result of which his back was injured leaving him paralysed. Otherwise, he was unscathed, so the Irvin suit which had trapped him also probably saved his life. Sid had by this time regained some mobility and since the Aussie could do nothing for himself it fell to him virtually to look after the gunner single-handed, since the orderlies left him to himself.

After some three weeks in the hospital, Sid and John were told to prepare to move, which was fairly easy as they had nothing to take with them. After saying their farewells to Smithy, they were again accompanied by three guards and a sergeant as they were taken to the railway station at Tegelen for their journey to the aircrew interrogation camp at Frankfurt. Neither Sid nor John could walk too well and played on it by moving at a snail's pace. This annoyed the guards very much and no matter how they screamed and shouted they continued to play on their injuries. Eventually, one of the guards, in frustration, picked up Sid and carried him to the train.

In company with the four Germans in the compartment the journey in the train seemed interminable as they made their way along the Rhine. It became almost a pattern for the train to go quite fast for ten minutes and then stop for ten minutes for most of the day and then make good time until it arrived at a small town on the Rhine. After this, the train kept going fairly well, although slowing down at small sidings, where it was possible to see the effects of the Allied bombing. Travelling down the Rhine was something always to be remembered by Sid. The beauty of the vineyards and castles on the slopes interspersed with market gardens growing vegetables but the true value of the bombing campaign became obvious as they travelled through the small towns which had very few buildings standing, rubble piled on the sides of the roads and pavements to keep the roads clear. Going through Cologne it seemed that only the cathedral was standing and everywhere they had visual evidence of the devastation wrought by the bombers. The whole journey was stop/go and they passed a huge pile of crashed Allied aircraft being collected to be re-smelted for the German aircraft industry.

Reaching Cologne they were shunted into the remains of a siding with lines uprooted and twisted and with craters in profusion where the rails used to be. Here they stayed for hours with their guards showing utter boredom until at last the train started its journey to Frankfurt at a speed less than walking pace, such was the effect of the bombing on the German transport system. Arriving in the middle of the night, time didn't appear to be very important to the Germans at this stage, John and Sid were transported in another gas-fuelled bus to a country mansion commandeered by the military. Here the beds were huge, with very deep feather mattresses, and Sid commented that he had never slept before or since in such a comfortable bed and envied the German gentry. There was an American here they regarded with some suspicion who claimed to have been shot down that day: his hand was bandaged and held in front of his shirt to act as a sling. His moans, groans and swearing kept the two of them awake for some considerable time but finally they dropped off and made up for the twenty hours they had been kept travelling. Later in the morning they were once more put on the gas-propelled bus and taken on to Dulag Luft. Again they were presented with the same old Red Cross form, of which the Germans apparently had an endless supply, and once more they filled in their name, rank and number. This was the last time the two were together as John was taken to the NCO compound and Sid to the officers'.

Surprisingly, Sid was not interrogated by the Luftwaffe but received a grilling from the senior British officer and his committee, who seemed not only more interested in his marital status than anything else, but also any information that might be useful to the Allies, position of aircraft, loaded wagon movements, etc. He was then given a packet of twenty Players, a bowl of hot soup along with a slice of black bread which was a little more palatable than previously as it was spread with Red Cross butter. Sid was then allocated a bed, issued with an ironstone china mug and spoon, together with a blanket, and was told that he could expect to be moved at any time of night or day. There were very little washing facilities and, even if there had been any, no towels were supplied. A bowl of hot soup was issued at lunchtime with a third of a loaf of black bread which had to last for three days. Little conversation took place between the prisoners because of the air of suspicion as to who was a friend or a German plant.

In due course, Sid and three other aircrew, in the company of four guards and the inevitable sergeant were entrained for a prison camp. The railway truck in which they were to travel had an abundance of straw on one side to be occupied by the guards but the other side was just bare boards so that the prisoners needed to rely entirely on their blanket for warmth and comfort. After being informed that their destination was Stalag Luft 3 at Sagan, they then started on a nightmarish journey, being left in sidings for hours at a time to allow other trains to pass and crawling along when actually moving. The only consolation was being let out of the truck when in sidings to allow for personal comforts, which the guards also took advantage of, as there were no water or toilet facilities on the train. They arrived at Sagan station forty-eight hours after leaving Dulag Luft.

Having to walk from the station to the camp was quite a chore for Sid as his ankle had swollen and got worse as he walked. This had not been helped by the long time in the truck and all four prisoners had to walk very slowly with the guards swearing and shouting at them all the way. On arrival at the camp, they were greeted by the commandant with the time-honoured words, "For you the war is over", before being stripped, searched, and again being invited to complete the same bogus form which they had failed several times to fill in before. Handed over to the SBO and his committee, Sid was again interrogated on his marital status and service career before being supplied with more cigarettes, a Red Cross parcel and then allocated a bed in one of the huts. With nearly fifty hours since sleeping properly he hit the pillow and went out like a light until awakened by another inmate with a piece of toasted black bread, this time with margarine and a slither of jam, a cup of Nescafe with sugar and milk from a tin of Klim. This was the first cup of what really tasted like coffee; in fact, a very acceptable breakfast, even though it was small. This was the only type of breakfast he was to get for the rest of the time he was a POW.

When summoned for Appel, (head count), Sid was informed, with others, that he was to be transferred to a satellite camp at Belaria, about 3km along the road. By now he had acquired another blanket, a Red Cross parcel, more cigarettes and other odds and bobs, so, rolling as much as possible in the blankets and spreading the rest about his person he set off, feeling like an itinerant rag and bone merchant. The walk turned out quite well with everyone taking their time. The weather was glorious and the guards did not appear over anxious to get to the other camp so the journey lasted over two hours. Arriving at Belaria they were met by a feldwebel who spoke with an Irish accent more Irish than the Irish, probably a repatriated fifth columnist. He normally took charge of the Appel and then disappeared for the rest of the day. Sid was welcomed by the SBO and committee and again went through the interrogation on his marital status, service career and names of people with whom he had served: it was always essential to ensure that they had no German plants in the camp.

The allocation of a billet came next and Sid found himself with six other officers in a room with accommodation for twelve. One of these, Flight Lieutenant George Newbury, had been a Spitfire pilot based at Malta who, on his first raid on the mainland of Italy was sweeping so low that a soldier fired a rifle at him and had the luck to puncture the cooling system of his Merlin engine so that, after twelve months of training, he was brought down on his first operation. After spending four years as a POW he stayed in the service at the end of the war and retired after twenty years with the rank of group captain. Of the others, one was a flight engineer, Flying Officer Ray Grayson, who had survived the Dams raid in 1943, and the only other Englishman was a Hurricane pilot by the name of Heywood who had been shot down somewhere over France and had been a POW for over a year. The other three were a Scottish navigator from a Lancaster and two Canadians, both fighter pilots, who were long time POWs.

Sid was surprised to find quite a number of prisoners there who were known to him from his days with 10 Squadron when they were shot down during his first tour of operations. One of them, a Canadian, gave him 200 Sweet Caporal cigarettes and with those already received he felt more than overloaded, particularly as he didn't smoke, but was told that the situation wouldn't last long and, anyway, they were good currency. As time went on, Sid got introduced to an American air gunner who swore as much as the one he met earlier in the mansion near Frankfurt and came to the conclusion that this must have been a common method of communication among American aircrew.

One day, Joe Hounam, Stan Somerscales' bomb aimer from their first tour on 'Shiny Ten' arrived at the camp and was allocated to a room which was occupied by South Africans, who all spoke English but, as soon as Joe entered the room, switched to Afrikaans. This was something which Joe found hard to live with so made application to transfer to Sid's room which still had bed space and, when granted, made the compliment up to nine. The days were spent playing cricket, hockey, football, or whatever sport was going on; walking round the circuit being another popular pastime which meant going round the perimeter of the camp inside the trip wire. This was set about eight to ten feet inside the main fence, the space in-between being a strictly no go area with any infringement likely to be death by shooting from the guards.

At night the windows and shutters of the huts were closed with lights switched off at ten. It was at this time that Sid's group often played bridge using lights manufactured from shallow meat paste tins as containers for melted margarine with a piece of string as a wick. While these improvised lamps gave light, they also produced a lot of smoke which, with the smoke from cigarettes, made the atmosphere in the room pretty foul. George Newbury had taught Sid the rudiments of bridge and on the basis of that the two partnered each other for the rest of the time in captivity.

Each room had been allotted a small piece of ground in which to grow vegetables, the seeds coming from the Red Cross: this was of great help to the inmates (kriegies) as it supplemented the German rations which were not always forthcoming. The winter of 1944/45 was so severe that the vegetable patches had to be abandoned so the Canadians flooded the area to use for ice skating. The cold was so intense the water could be seen to be freezing as soon as it hit the ground, thirty degrees below freezing being the normal temperature. Many of the Canadians were long serving prisoners and had skates and boots sent to them via the Red Cross. The speed and energy they put into their skating was unbelievable, one would think they had been living off the fat of the land rather than a near starvation diet. The severe gashes and cuts they sustained were horrific and, with no means of stitching them up, the doctor had his work cut out since, with no anaesthetics, and iodine as his only antiseptic, he was limited to tight bandages for treatment; and these were in short supply, so a line full of washed bandages was a common sight.

During the late summer of 1944 the Germans needed the space provided by the sports field to build more accommodation for the ever-increasing number of air force prisoners. Under the Geneva Convention they had an obligation to provide recreational facilities for POWs and so instigated walks around the countryside for prisoners prepared to sign a parole that they would not escape while so doing. To the best of Sid's knowledge everybody signed as it was such a thrill to walk outside of the wire and, anyway, enabled would-be escapers to sound out the lie of the land. All the workmen building these huts wore white overalls and only one guard was employed patrolling the ground between the compound and the building site. At twelve noon each day work stopped and, along with the guard, the workmen went to the canteen for lunch. One day, Wing Commander Tuck who had been moved in from Sagan just before the Great Escape, was observed wearing a pair of white pyjamas over his uniform and, as the workmen moved off for lunch, he tacked himself on behind the guard and continued to walk on past the gate as the workmen turned into the canteen. On down the road he walked but luck was not with him this day. A guard, who knew him well, was returning from the village, recognized him, and marched him straight back to the camp and a spell in the cooler. An immediate parade was ordered for a head count to be taken which took about two hours. These diversions were always well taken by the inmates for it kept the guards busy and in full kit with rifles during the count. Tuck had not expected to escape anyway but it provided the frustration and annoyance to the Germans he had planned.

*   *   *

On the evening of Sunday, 29th January 1945 the camp had gone through the routine of bedding down for the night when, in the early hours, around one o'clock, of the Monday morning there was bags of whistle-blowing and goons in full marching kit burst into the huts screaming "Raus, Raus", and paraded everyone outside the huts. When all were assembled the announcement was made that the camp was to be evacuated and that all prisoners were to be ready for a long march within the hour; rumour had it that the Russians were expected within the week. Pandemonium ensued as, with no one prepared for this turn of events, everybody attempted to pack as much food and kit as possible before it was time to parade again at 2:00 a.m. The Canadians had stacked thousands of packets of cigarettes and set them ablaze on the basis that if they couldn't carry them they were not going to leave them for the goons.

Again the parade was dismissed after being told to be ready to march off at 9:00 a.m. With thick snow on the ground up to six foot deep, Sid's mess of twelve, including five Americans, three Canadians and four Brits, decided that a little ingenuity was required to deal with the immediate future. Not every pilot officer has the opportunity to have a collection of majors, captains and flight lieutenants to work as his labourers but with Sid acting as designer and engineer in chief everyone fell to with a will in ripping out bed

boards and fashioning them into sledges. While his assistants were
straightening the nails Sid hurriedly put together three sledges each
of which had to be shared by a group of four, made up by four
Americans, three Americans and one Canadian, and four Brits. Each
sledge had to carry a share of the communal rations, blankets for
four, four Red Cross parcels which the Germans had distributed
weighing 7lb each, plus all the kit that each member had decided to
bring. It is probable that with an average of around 50lb per man
each sledge was loaded with about 2cwt and items for ready use such
as toilet, towels and washing facilities were carried by the airmen on
their backs. Fortunately, with the snow on the road some three feet
deep and rock hard the sledges ran fairly easily.

The march began just after 9:00 a.m. and, with the weight being
pulled, the three groups thanked their lucky stars that they had had
time to construct the sledges. Although very cold, the back packs and
pulling the sledges kept everyone warm. The guards were all old
pioneer type soldiers whose hardest task was carrying their own
packs and rifles, let alone guarding the POWs. Escape would have
been fairly easy but there was safety in numbers for to be caught
between the advancing Russians and the retreating Germans was not
a healthy situation to seek out. That first day, after walking for eight
hours and covering 20km, they arrived in a village called Kunau
where they were billetted in barns. Using their small stoves made
from Klim tins which they had brought with them from the camp,
the first thing on arrival was to boil water and make coffee with
Nescafe, Klim milk powder and sugar from the Red Cross parcels.
Sid and his friends then lit fires and with the help of tins from the
parcels were able to make a fairly substantial meal. After the long
walk in the awful conditions everyone removed their boots, which
were soaking wet, buried them in the straw to prevent them freezing
up and, although wet through, slept until milking time. Breakfast
was the norm, a slice of bread and jam and a cuppa, without the
benefit of fresh milk which Sid had hoped to scrounge. Appel was
called and the march resumed at 9:00 a.m.

There had been no facilities for washing or shaving and as Sid said, "We looked a motley collection of tramps and with pulling our sledges, having all sorts of tins, utensils and other items tied round our belts and, with strips of cloth acting as puttees tied round our legs to keep us warm, we must have looked like a real 'Fred Karno's Air Force'". The civilians along the road were very good, producing hot water for making coffee or tea and even parted with potatoes, vegetables and sometimes the odd egg, in exchange for cigarettes. The old volkesturmer guards didn't care a damn but the officers were dashing up and down on their horses screaming at the people and the guards that these men were terrorfliegers and thus the enemy, but nobody took any notice. It seemed that they knew the war was nearly over and were trying to make some recompense.

The route they covered during the day took the marchers through Wiesau before they eventually arrived at a farmyard near Gross Selton. The barns here were much cleaner and the flyers were able to snuggle down into the hay and get warm by the fires which were quickly under way using scraps of wood, of which there was a plentiful supply. The smell of cooking became all-pervading as the kriegies put together hot meals made from the Red Cross tins of stew and the vegetables they had collected on the way. It was very welcome as the Germans had provided no food to them for two days. The farmer went into a rage when he caught the prisoners using his electric lights to settle themselves down but was appeased by a packet of cigarettes, the usual way to sort out difficulties.

Awakened again at milking time the POWs were paraded for head count at 9:00 a.m. and told that they would be staying there for the day. Rumour ran riot. The Russians were three miles behind us; the Yanks and Brits had crossed the Rhine; Hitler was dead and Goering had taken over. Eventually the truth emerged. Owing to the fact that the group had closed up on the batch of prisoners ahead there was no accommodation available and therefore the group would have to stay put for twenty-four hours. This was very welcome in giving time to recuperate a little after the conditions they had been struggling with. During the day a motorized section of a Panzer division consisting of several lorries and a car of the commanding officer drew up, having been chased out of Litzmanstadt by the Russians. In the back of the officer's car was a large, fat, plucked goose which was left unattended while the officer set off to make arrangements for his troops. When he returned, the goose had vanished and a rather serious situation developed as these were not the type of troops to get mixed up with. The officer screamed at all and sundry, called for the senior British officer, who was a group captain, and threatened strong reprisals including shooting a number of prisoners unless the bird was returned. By this time, of course, the goose had long been cooked and eaten. A series of consultations and negotiations then ensued, at the end of which the Panzer officer was finally appeased with 100 cigarettes and a 4oz block of chocolate and, with the troops now more friendly and assuring them that the war would be over shortly, exchanges of German rations for cigarettes began to take place all around, followed by another hot meal.

The following morning after Appel, which had become a complete farce as the pioneer guards could never get the figures right and the oil in their typewriter had frozen up, the march resumed at 8:00 a.m. The guards had succumbed to the elements far more seriously than the prisoners with the likelihood that their rifles had also frozen up. The Americans and Canadians had been hived off to make for a different camp so that it was now almost a one hundred percent RAF contingent as they marched a further twenty kilometres through Tapperstadt and on to Birkenstadt. During the afternoon the temperature rose and while this was in some ways appreciated it made for much more effort to pull the sledge through the resultant mud and slush left by the melting snow. By now Sid was the only man fit to drag the sledge, his other three mates being in very poor condition. The barns where they halted for the night had no lights or heating with everywhere flooded and cow dung inches deep and no fires were able to be kindled. Sid got out his trusty stove again to brew up coffee for the four in his group and made a sandwich for each of them. The remaining bread they had was almost solid, so slicing was relatively easy, but a tin of fish paste which he opened together with the margarine resisted all attempts to be spread so the sandwiches just had solid lumps between the slices. Pretty ghastly, but better than nothing at all.

They were bedded down and locked in the barns by 7:00 p.m. for what was to be a very hard night. Sid had become a nurse to his other three comrades who, with a number of other prisoners were in a sad state and now suffering from diarrhoea. With no light, no toilets, no running water, the conditions were almost unimaginable, with moans and groans arising from all over the barn throughout the night and it was for everyone a relief to see the morning light.

There was further relief as the Germans distributed a fifth of a loaf of bread to each of them, it being the first rations of any kind issued since leaving Belaria some five days earlier: it was at the same time announced that the day would be spent at the farm due to parties ahead slowing down leaving no accommodation on the road. Although the conditions were deplorable, the delay was welcomed by the prisoners as by now, due to the change of weather with a complete thaw, the sledges being used by many had now become unmanageable, so had to be dumped, the wood being very useful as fuel for fires. Sid counted himself lucky as he scrounged through the farm disposal area and came across an old pram which he was able to retrieve. Admittedly, it only had three wheels, all badly buckled, but after straightening these and fashioning a fourth wheel from a piece of plank from the same dump he now had a substitute conveyance. It did take Sid a considerable time but in the end, although pretty rough he had been able to square the pram up which allowed him and his three companions to load up all their goods previously carried on the sledge.

The next day they set off at the usual 9:00 a.m. The roads were dreadful, swimming with water and mud up to their ankles. Sid found the pram really punishing to push with no option but to struggle on as his other three compatriots were, by this time, so ill that they were being carried in the Red Cross cart which accompanied the contingent. It was a surprise to him that they did not contract pneumonia. He was now falling further and further behind the column with the strain of keeping the heavily-loaded pram moving, a job for a fit man, not a half-starved kriegie of under nine and a half stone but, in spite of the continual heckling of "Raus, Raus," he ignored the German guards and still kept going as best he could. Staggering up the main street through a village called Muskau, disaster struck, the homemade wheel finally disintegrating. The street was full of housewives who commenced jeering which soon stopped as Sid unloaded some heavy boots and threw them in the gutter which started a melee as the women scrambled for them. Now with slightly less weight but with only three wheels Sid wrestled with the pram to push on for a further kilometre, eventually conceding defeat as it was beyond his endurance to carry on. He sat down on the pram wondering what to do and waited for the reaction of his guards. After much screaming and shouting they settled the problem by recalling the Red Cross cart and throwing the remains of the pram and its contents on the back. By this time the rest of the column was out of sight and the cart then galloped off to catch up, leaving Sid and the two guards to meander onwards on their own. They eventually arrived at their destination to be reunited with the marchers at a hamlet named Schonheide, where Sid, before doing anything else, had to collect the contents of the pram and distribute them between the four members of his clutch and make provision for transportation the next day. Finally, he brewed up a hot drink for the four of them and shared out a packet of cracker biscuits with a little margarine before preparing to settle down in a damp, strawless, unlit barn housing one hundred men. The doors were locked so there were no means of making a hot meal and although a hard dirt floor was not the ideal for dreamless sleep Sid was so exhausted with the struggles of the day that, as soon as he hit his makeshift pillow, he went into oblivion for twelve hours.

The column was only on the road for about an hour the next day before arriving at a tank corps depot where, locked in an empty tank shed, they were supplied with a large barrel of soup. Sufficient for half a litre per man, it was a colourless liquid with no solids and with a faint smell of cereals. It was the first hot food supplied by their captors since leaving Belaria some seven days earlier.

After this break the column was re-formed, marched off to a nearby railway siding and at around 4:30 p.m. loaded on a train and locked in with fifty men to a truck. It was impossible for everyone to lie down at the same time so a rota had to be followed to enable some rest, although sleep was out of the question with no straw to cushion the bare boards of the wagons. Seven hours later the train commenced its journey and crawled along for an hour before being shunted into a siding to allow other movements of trains. This pattern continued throughout the night, which in some ways was a relief, as the goons allowed the POWs to disembark, one truck at a time, for personal comfort, they also availing themselves of the same opportunities as there were no toilets on the train. Eventually the train arrived at Luckenwalde station, the prisoners having been informed earlier that this was their destination and, after the hardships of the previous week, they considered that covering sixty kilometres in the last twenty-four hours had not been such bad going.

Darkness was falling as the train arrived and the goons had a hard time counting the prisoners so that, after four attempts with different results, they gave up and marched them to the nearby camp. During the march it started to drizzle with rain so that by the time they reached the camp everyone was soaking wet which didn't seem to worry the Germans who kept their charges standing around in the rain until 8:00 p.m. before admitting them into the forlager where they were searched and de-loused before finally being housed in barracks at 8:00 a.m. the following morning. After Sagan, the POWs found utter chaos in the accommodation: the doors would not close, holes in the linoleum, large patches of damp from the broken windows, bunks three-tiered in batches of twelve and filthy torn mattresses with very little straw in the fillings. The water had been turned off in the German forlager so washing and cooking facilities were non-existent and the general consensus was that the camp had previously housed slave labour. By now, everyone was almost out on their feet not having slept for about fifty hours, so Sid, having made a hot brew on his trusty little stove and doled out a couple of biscuits apiece to the rest of his quartet, lay down and slept for eighteen hours, waking up with every bone aching in his body.

The SBO and his committee were soon on the ball. The barrack blocks became a hive of industry with German workers repairing windows, doors, etc. The stoves in the centres of the rooms were supplied with fuel and soon glowing which dried the rooms pretty quickly. Water was restored, although somewhat limited as the plumbing was very weak and unable to take any pressure. The temperature for the first two or three weeks never lifted above zero but it was not unusual to see a man, stripped naked by the hydrant in the middle of the parade ground, having a sponge down, using a klim tin as his only receptacle to contain the water; and it took a brave man to strip off in those temperatures. The toilets consisted of two long benches divided by a partition, each bench having twelve holes and for washing, twelve filthy, rusty bowls which had not been used for ages hung on one of the walls.

In the compound at Luckenwalde were the Norwegian army's complete complement of officers, led by General Otto Ruge, about five hundred in all, two huts were occupied by Polish officers and further blocks contained 500 American air force officers, all their conditions similar to those found by the RAF contingent. Within a month the SBO had transformed the place beyond anyone's wildest dreams. Sid accompanied George Newbury into an American hut to visit an airman who George had known in captivity in Italy. Apparently, the Americans had been there for a month before the RAF arrived and had been unable to get any changes made so were highly delighted with the upgrading that had been achieved. They were also dependent on the hot soup the Germans supplied each day, this being the only hot food they had, that is, until the RAF kriegies introduced them to the little Klim stoves they had manufactured. Tickled pink with the simplicity of them, for the next week or two the Americans' main occupation was tin-bashing as they set out to copy the stoves. During the next two weeks Red Cross parcels started to arrive and these were issued one per week to each man, making the meals more appetising as the German issue of food was very rough and only at a level to prevent the prisoners from starving. Each American kept the parcel to himself, whereas the RAF formed themselves into messes of twelve having a hot meal each day; so, if a tin of corned meat was opened, it being too much for one man, by the mess system the tin was shared between twelve men together with any potatoes and vegetables available, thus allowing rations to be spread out equally with nothing wasted. The Yanks soon cottoned on to and appreciated the system.

The escape committee now began to plan special meals which could be cooked and saved against the day when the Germans pulled out leaving the POWs to fend for themselves: this was anticipated to be not too long in the future. There was a delay in setting up the radio and getting the BBC as the equipment had been split up between members of the committee when Belaria was evacuated and it was taking time to gather it all together as strict secrecy had to be maintained. Eventually, the first news was disseminated and was well received: the war was going well for the Allies, having crossed the Rhine in the west and being in constant engagement with the enemy. The committee decided to let the Americans have a copy of the news but were in complete consternation when they observed an American colonel, standing on a chair, reading it out to all and sundry. Had there been ferrets around there was a chance that the radio would have been found and confiscated.

Sid was visiting the Americans with George when news of an American setback came through. This produced gloom and despondency among the American prisoners who began to make bets on the war lasting another year. George, without thinking, put his foot well and truly in it by assuring them that there was no need to worry, they just had to send for Monty and his batman who would have it contained within a week. Sid did not realise that he could still run so fast as the situation became really dangerous for the two of them, the Yanks looking for blood. They decided to give Karl, George's friend, a wide birth until things had died down. Another day, in mid-April, the sirens sounded but, as it was noon and a warm day, most of the prisoners were outside which prompted the Germans to order them inside. There was no response and although the guards screamed and shouted at them it made no difference, for this was a show the kriegies were not going miss. The thrill of seeing the masses of Flying Fortresses escorted by fighters with no Luftwaffe aircraft to be seen was a morale-booster, bringing with it the hope that the sands were rapidly running out for the Reich. Sid and the others watched as sky markers were released and the Fortresses changed course but either the wind was in the wrong direction or it was an incendiary raid for no explosions were heard before they watched the return of the planes and cheered themselves hoarse. When it was all over, the Yanks were positively strutting around, saying, 'that's the way the Americans do it', and the RAF had to admit that it was a very impressive show.

That same night the RAF were having a band concert in one of their huts when the air raid alert again sounded off, and although the lights were extinguished immediately, the band continued to play until there was an almighty bang, the windows rattled, and it seemed as though the hut had been lifted off its foundations. Then there was silence for a short time except for bodies falling on the floor, scraping to get under the bunks before all hell let loose; the noise was terrifying with great flashes in the sky and the assembly were much relieved when in due course it ended. The silence was almost uncanny and no one had any more interest in the band as the lights came on. Fires could be seen through the window and they, together with different versions of what had happened, kept conversation going for hours. Next day it was the turn of the RAF contingent to hold their heads high with, 'that's the way the Brits do it', and the Americans, who had been overwhelmed with the display, agreed they had been frightened out of their wits, as had everybody in the camp, but said that it must have been a thousand bomber raid. The BBC news stated that it was Potsdam which had been raided, first by 750 American Fortresses during the day and then by 500 Lancasters at night.

It was evident that the war could not last much longer, the German guards were on edge and the warning went around not to provoke them. The camp band concerts had now become, more or less, a nightly performance with few prisoners bothering with bridge or other diversions. This particular night there was a band concert in Sid's hut, normally occupied by 200 men but which now had some 500 crammed in. Sid had been suffering from a tummy bug and, shortly after the concert began, had to leave and make for the toilet block. In his own words:

> "Examining the bench by the light of a match, there were no lights in the block, I located myself, dropped the match through the hole, and sat down. Almost immediately, there was an almighty bang and a sheet of flame. I pulled up my slacks and dashed outside to see a funnel of flame shooting out of the chimney. I dashed back to my hut and shouted, 'The bogs are on fire'. The band and its audience poured outside and started cheering, while the band re-formed in a circle and led the singing of that old well-known ditty, 'Please don't burn our s.... house down, Father has promised to pay...'. I doubt whether it's ever been sung with such feeling. It was all very amusing, but I then was a little scared of repercussions from the Germans, but they did nothing and we had to share the Polish toilets from thereon."

Clearly it was obvious that the Germans were now making plans to call it a day, the guards having been reduced with no ferrets around anymore. The defence system, organized by the defence committee for when the Germans departed, was reviewed and brought up-to-date and everyone warned not to antagonize them. Unfortunately, the officers' compound had no contact with the nearby other ranks' compound where the same discipline was not being shown. The night before the Germans pulled out, two Canadian NCOs decided to escape by going through the wire as the security was so slack, but did not count on the guards in the goon boxes who had not been relieved. When the Canadians were caught in the wire one of these guards fired and killed both of them. Another twenty-four hours and they would have been free. On the morning of 21st April the Germans prepared to leave as they de-manned the goon boxes, and the sentries and guards although still on duty, were in full battledress and had withdrawn to the forlager. At noon they paraded in full marching order, at the same time the commandant sending for General Ruge, the most senior Allied officer in the camp. The general could not immediately be located and, with the Germans in such a haste to depart, they formally handed over the camp to the most senior-looking officer they could find, who happened to be an American, before marching off and out of the prisoners' lives.

The defence arrangements immediately came into force with everybody advised not to venture out of the camp as no Allied forces were yet in evidence and the militia and Hitler Youth forces were in the woods surrounding the camp. At around 6:00 a.m. the next morning a Russian tank came charging down the main road of the camp tearing down the barbed wire fence which, caught in the tracks, became very dangerous to anyone in the vicinity as the wire and posts were dragged along by the tank. It eventually stopped and everyone crowded around for a while until the Russian prisoners in the camp were invited to follow the tank into Luckenwalde. The remaining barbed wire was now a problem as the tank had really churned up the road and the fence was entangled all the way along. The rest of the day for all the officers was taken up with clearing the wire and making the road fit for use, which was heavy going for undernourished men not used to manual labour.

The following day, a fleet of trucks arrived led by a General Famin to take the remaining Russian prisoners on to Berlin with them. General Famin remained and called General Ruge into his office while they sorted out the administration of the camp. The SBO was put in charge along with his committee now containing some Americans who had been enrolled, General Famin then departed taking General Ruge, the Norwegian, with him. The committee organized teams to go out and scrounge around for food as the Russians lived off the land and had no food to give to prisoners, who they despised anyway, their motto being, 'to fight until dead, as a prisoner is as good as dead anyway'.

About a week after they left, some of the former German guards returned and surrendered to the Senior British Officer, hoping to be classed as POWs of the British. This seemed to be quite a laugh as the former prisoners now appeared to be just as much prisoners of the Russians as they had been of the Germans, apart from not suffering from having boarded windows or 'lights out'; although there was no electricity for about five days, anyway. The Germans were handed over to the Russians and that was the last seen of them.

Eventually permission was given for the camp inmates to walk outside the camp. On one side of the road was a wood containing a small lake into which the Russians would throw hand grenades and, having collected sufficient of the resulting dead fish for themselves, allow the balance to be collected by the airmen and taken to the camp kitchen to be added to the daily soup. After a few days of this, Sid and George while out walking came across a pair of feet sticking out from the undergrowth in the wood which, on investigation, proved to be a Russian ex-prisoner who had died from malnutrition. Someone must have known he was there as his boots had been removed, but even so, after they had reported his presence to the Russians, it was nearly a week before the body was removed. There were often frightening confrontations with the Russian Army personnel. Some of the RAF officers had managed to retain their Air Ministry watches and when out walking in the wood were waylaid by the Russians who relieved them of the watches at gunpoint. By the time they had got their protest through the Russian hierarchy, who ordered that if it happened again the culprit would be shot, it was too late as there were no more watches left to be stolen. For the most part the watches were of little use to the Russians who could not read or tell the time. It was usual for Russian guards to be on the gate of the camp but no one knew why, as they never stopped or checked anyone and were never relieved, change only taking place when a guard came back in drunk and was conned by the existing one to take his place.

The Germans were still in the vicinity for about a week before the last of the firing was heard and the foraging parties were not very successful in finding any food in quantity. One evening, the airmen were called upon to unload a number of trucks reputed to contain food. The first one was dealt with fairly quickly, it contained a dozen pigs each of which, as it came down the ramp, had a gun put to its ear and was shot by a waiting Russian before having its throat cut by a second soldier. Other troops then carried the carcasses in turn to a blazing fire where they were thrown on to burn off the hair before being put on a table for butchering. The rest of the trucks contained salt. German children came to the camp begging for food as there was none in the shops and they and their parents must have been starving but, when seen by the Russians, they were chased away. However, the former airmen did share as must as possible with the children although they themselves were little better off. The foraging parties had managed to get some potatoes and vegetables and the bakery had been coaxed into activity again although the black bread was worse than it had been previously: but on the basis that beggars cannot be choosers it was a question of managing with what was available. Quarters were now a little better in that the German officers' accommodation and offices had been given to the airmen to use and while some had beds, others had to bed down on tables and chairs, but this was better than they had been used to.

About ten days after being overrun by the Russians a convoy of American trucks arrived to take out as many of the American and British officers as they could on the trucks, but the Russians refused to allow this to go ahead as they had received no orders for the evacuation. All the Americans were disarmed and sent back to wherever they had come from. It was a great disappointment to all the ex-prisoners whose hopes had risen to the sky at the sight of the American trucks. Still no food was issued on a regular basis by the Russians and although one of Sid's messmates trapped a large hare which was cooked and shared out, it was something which Sid, even though ravenous and half-starving, could not face, as even the smell of rabbit cooking had always turned his stomach. Another ten days were to pass before it was announced that the airmen were to be repatriated, this time in Russian transport, which proved to be captured German vehicles. From experience they knew they could not expect any food from the Russians so the remainder of the food was packed up for the journey.

Early the next morning, after as big a breakfast as they could eat, the airmen were loaded fifty to a truck and started off towards Leipzig, gratefully taking their last look at Luckenwalde. The journey was a nightmare, the drivers being inexperienced and having no idea how to handle the trucks. There were delays due to breakdowns, the roads were at times almost impassable with diversions because of blown-up bridges and crawling along dried up water courses became a norm. As expected no food was supplied and no drinks made available. It was 4:00 p.m. before the convoy arrived at the rendezvous with the Americans who had given up expecting them and were just about to leave, having been told that the meeting was at 1:30 p.m. At long last there was a feeling of safety among the group at being in American hands but there was still a long way to go to their destination of the airfield at Halle near Leipzig. The journey from thereon was not much better than the previous eight hours, only the American drivers were a lot better than the Russians, doing their best to get back to their base as quickly as possible, arriving at around 9:00 p.m. All the American staff had also given up on the convoy getting there for the night so everywhere was locked up and the canteen closed. This was quite a blow, as the men had had nothing to eat except the little food they carried and certainly nothing to drink since leaving Luckenwalde early that morning. Nobody on the camp seemed to have any idea what to do, so the ex-prisoners took the law into their own hands, broke into the canteen, eating the next day's ration of bread which was white and after their previous diet tasted like cake, slaked their thirst, before being allocated beds and snuggling down to a glorious sleep.

Everyone was still filthy and unshaven but the next morning after a typical American breakfast of pancakes and honey, Sid and the RAF contingent boarded American Dakotas and were flown to a British air base at Brussels. Here, after being de-bugged and having a bath, shave and shampoo, Sid felt clean for the first time since being shot down fourteen months earlier. True, there had been showers in the camps he had been in but these were only once a week and the best wash was accomplished by removing a tap out of the cold water line and having the full force of the water hitting the body. The Germans took a dim view of the use of water in this way, so it could only be done when there were no ferrets in the offing and, even so, had its limitations as it did not allow for the body to be soaped first and was extremely cold. Sid remembered Christmas 1944 when an Australian air gunner bet a friend that he would stand under one such shower for ten minutes in exchange for a day's food ration. The bet was accepted, although the doctor decreed that he was not to have the water directed at his head and, with the bath house crowded to capacity with onlookers, the show went ahead. When the ten minutes had been counted out, the Aussie had to be carried to his hut and thawed out gradually – but he had won his bet!

After the cleansing at the Brussels camp, Sid and his comrades were given clean clothing, battledress, and a medical examination before being taken to the mess for an enormous meal, (by their recent standards, anyway), following which, they were whisked into a hotel with a comfortable bed for the night. They had also been issued with about £10.00 in Belgian money so, before turning in, decided a night in Brussels was in order and although inevitably ending up in a bar, they were unable to drink very much, running out of cash fairly quickly.

The next day they were flown back to England in the fuselage of a Lancaster, not enjoyed very much by Sid after the spaciousness of the Halifaxes which gave more freedom to the crews to move around. Landing at Northolt, they were again de-bugged, shaved, bathed and given a haircut, then a full medical before a trip to the mess for a welcome meal. Sid took the opportunity to send a telegram to Violet, his wife, to say that he would be home within the next week but was taken by surprise when summoned to the adjutant's office, where he was issued with a leave pass, some money and a first class rail pass to Manchester. Considering that over a thousand were repatriated that day the organization was quite remarkable. Catching the first available train, Sid arrived at London Road Station, Manchester at around 7:00 p.m., quite a different train journey than the last one he had taken: three and a half hours to travel 180 miles as against twenty-four hours to travel sixty miles in Germany. Picking up a taxi in Manchester to run him to his home in Eccles, Sid paid the driver on the way and asked him not to stop outside his house, merely to slow down to allow him to jump out and get into the house without being seen. He was quite sure that nobody saw him arrive but at 10:30 p.m. there was a knock at the door, which, when opened, let in half the customers from his local, The White Horse, one with a nine gallon cask of beer on his shoulder, with everyone else, including the landlord and landlady, carrying a bottle of spirits or wine in their pocket. Sid became hopelessly drunk but, at last, he was home with his wife and newly-born daughter after the hardships of the last year or so.

* * *

Sid Stephen's parachute was buried in a box by the farmer about twenty feet from his house. For two weeks Boers was exasperated by the Germans who came every day searching all around the farm for it: parachutes were always a perk for the troops to send home to their families for clothing. After the liberation it was dug up and, for many years, parts of the parachute were used to make clothing for the Boers family.

In 1992 whilst taking a photograph of the farm, Lockerplei, on the author's behalf, Leo Pierey was approached by a lady walking in the garden. She asked him, "Why do you photograph our house, why are you interested?"

Leo: "For an English airman who landed here in 1944."

Lady: "Yes, I know. I have often heard that story. The aircraft crashed in the wood and that airman came to this farm."

Leo: "Your name is Boers?"

Lady: "Yes, my husband is the son of the farmer who picked up that Englishman."

Leo: "That man is still alive. He lives now in Australia."

Lady: "And his parachute still lies in our attic."

I was able to obtain the remains of that parachute in May 1993 and it is now lodged with the Yorkshire Air Museum at Elvington.

Chapter IX

In the Hands of the Enemy

After the time it had taken to escape from his turret it seemed only seconds before John Rowe came down to earth through a small clump of trees. John's own words can best tell what happened next:

> I tried to stand but couldn't. I knew my left knee was broken and the right one was badly bent. I pulled my 'chute out of the tree and covered it as far as possible. I was in a field and could see a hedge some 100 yards away. I crawled across the field and found a draining ditch into which I rolled and lay still. Within a few minutes there were several 'goons'[1] on bikes, plenty of shouting and whistle-blowing on the road only a few feet away. They appeared to be heading in the direction of the aircraft which I had heard blow-up and I could see the flames in the sky, probably only about quarter to half a mile away.
>
> When the road was clear, I crawled to a gate in the hedge and then across the road to a farmhouse which was virtually opposite. I reached the barn which was on the left hand side of the house to the right and went through the door of, what we call in Cornwall, the 'mowie', where all the pitchforks and tools were kept and there flopped down with my back to the door. Of course, being at the back end of the aircraft I wasn't even sure which country I was in –

---

[1] Probably Dutch ARP members since the Germans were not there until later.

could have been Holland, Belgium or Germany. I found I was bleeding from my forehead and, when I saw myself later in a mirror, my face was caked in a mask of blood.

About 5:00 a.m. a dog came, out of the farmhouse I presume, and started barking at the door. The farmer came and I opened the door. He was fairly old, as I recollect, short and grizzled. He helped me into the house, gave me a glass of stone-cold milk and a fat bacon sandwich and then cleaned me up a bit. A younger man appeared and later came back with one or two others. Then the local policeman came on the scene but the language difficulty still persisted. Eventually the local teacher was sent for and I was able to converse with him in French.

I'm a bit hazy about what went on after that – must have been the head injury, but, some considerable time after I remember being surrounded by German uniforms in a prison somewhere[2] and then being taken to Maastricht hospital. There were three of us in the ward, Doug Smith, an Aussie from Sydney, Sid Stephen and myself. We couldn't say too much in case the place was 'bugged' for information. Sid was cut, I think, by his 'chute harness which had been loose. I had both legs in plaster and Doug was in almost complete plaster – a broken spine I think.

From here I was taken in a hospital train down the banks of the Rhine to Tegelen where the opera house was a recuperation centre. A short stay here was followed by a journey to Dulag Luft for the usual interrogation treatment before being moved right across Germany, via Dresden to Luft 7 on the Polish border.

Life went on in the camp until early January 1945 when we were forced marched for nearly a month in front of the Russian advance. On one day we were kept going longer

---

[2] Actually Gulpen Police Station.

than usual in order to cross the Oder before the Germans blew the bridge at midnight.

It was twenty-six degrees below at one time and, of course, we never had the food or clothing to cope. We were lucky to find a barn at night otherwise we slept in the open. The German tanks were more or less making roads in the snow for us as they retreated. We finished up south of Potsdam, in a huge camp with a Russian compound holding thousands. The Russians eventually overran the camp but wouldn't release us for a couple of weeks, so we eventually escaped from them and got over the Elbe into Yank territory. The Americans worked us back to Brussels from where I flew home in a Lancaster. After repatriation leave I was at RAF Cosford Medical Centre but with my father's death in November I was given a Class B release in December. Never did finish the medical treatment!

* * *

Jack Reavill lay at the foot of a tree just inside the woods where the aircraft had crashed. He was suffering from multiple injuries, broken ribs, arms and legs and was unable to move. It was to be nearly seven hours that he would lay there, drifting in and out of consciousness, before assistance would become available. Jeu Van Wersch apparently rode up to the Wegelen woods between 7:00 and 8:00 a.m. and found Jack lying there. Realizing that there was little he could do, Jeu dropped his coat over Jack and then, untethering his horse, rode down to Mechelen to seek help. Here, on arrival he contacted Doctor Janssen who gave him to understand that headmaster Ortmans, the local chief of the Air Raid Precautions Service, had to be advised. A little later an ambulance car of sorts drove up to Hommerich and then to the end of the field. As the car could not proceed further, men went on foot to where Jack lay and he was carried to the vehicle on a farm gate used as an improvised stretcher. By about 9:00 a.m. he was lying on the floor in the hallway of a house in Mechelen and it was from here that he was taken into custody by the Germans. This is based on Jeu Van Wersch's account but other Dutchmen who claim to have been there have thrown doubt on Jeu's part in this as Jack was taken to a house near Wittem.

Most Allied aircrew captured by the Luftwaffe were treated correctly in accordance with the Geneva Convention. There was, of course, the camp where RAF NCO aircrew were kept in manacles, for nearly a year, I believe, but it is unlikely that this was a decision of the German air force. Jack Reavill was to have the misfortune to fall into the hands of what can only be described as a sadistic arm of the German armed forces.

It is believed that he was taken to the Blumenthal convent in Vaals where the three borders of Germany, Holland and Belgium meet. Blumenthal (Flower Valley) was in former times the castle-like home of an important textile manufacturer who supplied uniform material to Napoleon, among others. In 1850 it was taken over as a convent by the nuns of the Sacred Heart, who later added school buildings, and from then it was a boarding school for wealthy girls, mostly German, until it was commandeered during the war for use as an isolation hospital. The nuns were allowed to stay. In recent years the buildings have been demolished.

By the time Jack arrived here nearly ten hours must have elapsed since he had been blown out of the aircraft and, so far, he had received no attention to his injuries. His stretcher was placed on the floor a few feet away from an examination table and he was then joined by two members of the medical staff in white coats, one of whom was certainly a medical officer, who told him to get up on the table. The instruction was given in German and during the time Jack spent here no interpreter was brought in. If, in the circumstances, one could say there was an advantage then it was with the wireless operator since he could speak German and therefore understood what was being said without letting on that he understood. Indeed, he persisted in speaking only in English and "failing to understand" the questions and instructions thrown at him. With his injuries –

broken legs, ribs and arm, and multiple gashes – there was no way he could have lifted himself on to the table and, in spite of repeated commands accompanied by sign-language to do so he persisted in English to say that he could not lift himself. Eventually, he was put on the table.

Now the officer began his interrogation in response to which Jack gave his name, rank and number in accordance with the usual rules of warfare. He was then asked to give the names of his comrades to which Jack repeated his name, rank and number. The question was repeated several times, always receiving the same response, before the German tired of the game and added to the question that no attention would be given to Jack's injuries unless he gave the names of his comrades in the aircraft. Obviously the German knew that they had only accounted for five members of the crew. In spite of this threat, which he fully understood, Jack continued in only giving his name, rank and number in English but once or twice saying in very basic German that he did not understand German. Again and again his captor reiterated, always in German, that Jack would receive no sustenance or medical attention unless he answered. But Jack was made of pretty stern stuff and, in spite of the continual pain from his injuries, maintained his reply of name, rank and number only, to the point where the German was as good as his word. Apart from what was probably an anti-tetanus injection, given by one of the nuns, not even first aid treatment was administered nor even a drop of water given.

By mid-afternoon the German commandant realised he was getting nowhere with Jack and so had him put on a small open truck to be driven to Aachen station. On the way the army driver chattered away in German saying that his family lived in Aachen which meant that he would be able to visit them after driving to the station. About a week previously Bomber Command had made a very effective raid on Aachen which had caused much damage to the centre and south of the town and particularly to the roads and railway. When the driver began to realise the extent of the damage he almost went berserk, driving madly round the town over the damaged roads regardless of Jack being tossed about in the truck. Eventually his anger subsided and he reported to the railway station where Jack was handed over to our equivalent of the railway transport officer.

This particular officer made it clear almost immediately that he had two pet hates in life, Russians and American terrorfliegers. Jack was put into the second category and instructions given to several officer cadets assisting the RTO to parade him up and down the platforms on a stretcher as an American terrorflieger to all passengers emerging from arriving trains. After the RTO had tired of this particular exercise he was then put on a train to Cologne where he was again disembarked and placed behind the counter of the station cafeteria while awaiting further transport. Here, the German counter assistant showed some compassion by taking a wet cloth to clean some of the caked blood from his face before he was again entrained, this time to Bonn. It was from here that he was driven to Siegburg, a small village then on the outskirts of Bonn, to be put in a prison of the Napoleonic era, standing in the shadow of the castle.

The prison housed slave labour from France, Russia and Italy in the main, although it might be mentioned that the French, about two hundred of them, were volunteers who answered Petain's call for Frenchmen to assist the Führer in building the new greater Europe. Most of the inmates went out of the camp to work, mainly on agriculture, and while the Russians and Italians were well-guarded the number of guards looking after the French was almost minimal. After arrival his injuries received some attention from a doctor with the Russian prisoners to the extent of being bound up in paper bandages but, nevertheless, having no dressing on the wounds. Apart from a German surgeon in the hospital at Siegburg castle each of the three main nationalities had a doctor of their own ilk looking after them and this was fortunate for Jack since it brought the Russian doctor, 'Boris', into contact with him.

For two weeks Boris looked after him, doing what he could, but seriously hampered by lack of equipment and general medical facilities. He pressed the commandant to send Jack to the hospital for urgent attention, since his condition was deteriorating, but was led to understand that 'it was verboten to operate on terrorfliegers' and that Boris would be executed if he continued to give medical aid to the terrorflieger. Nevertheless Boris continued his ministrations, albeit surreptitiously. It would appear that the camp commander must be seen, even in the best light, as a sadist, for he waited a full two weeks before he sent Jack to the hospital and then only when he knew the German surgeon had gone on leave. The result? A botched job by what were unqualified army medical students, following which they amputated a foot. Without the continual visits or care by Boris, in spite of the death threat, there must be some doubt as to whether Jack would have ever left that camp alive. Certainly, his other leg was undoubtedly saved by the Russian's action, although later, the German surgeon came into the picture and treated Jack ethically and correctly.

During the hot summer of that year Jack continued to be incarcerated with nine other inmates in a cell of about thirteen by eleven feet with no ventilation whatsoever so that he was having to lie as close as possible to the stone walls in order to breathe cold air off the wall. To get fresh air he had to rely on other prisoners to carry him outside to lay on the ground which was rare, until, following the Arnhem operation, as the months wore on, two Americans and a British sergeant paratrooper were put into the prison camp. By what means the Germans selected Jack and the other three to be imprisoned in this hell-hole is unfathomable. They were all legitimate prisoners of war and should have been held in a recognized Allied POW camp. Certainly they were not held incommunicado since Jack was writing to his parents in July and then began to receive Red Cross parcels without which he would have starved. At one stage a German prisons inspector was due to visit the camp and Jack made it known that he would make the inspector aware of the situation in the camp and of his own in particular. Several people warned him that if he spoke up it would be unlikely that he would survive to leave the prison. Consequently when he was approached and questioned by the inspector he had to say that his treatment and everything else in the place was fine. This in itself must have been a galling experience for him to have to submit himself. But there was no doubt in his mind that the advice had to be heeded.

Sometime, probably late in October, the International Red Cross were due to visit the prison to inspect the conditions under which the prisoners-of-war were being held and certainly there was no way Jack intended to keep quiet, since they were acting on behalf of the protecting power. Somehow his intentions were betrayed, it is thought by one of the Italians, and, at last, he suddenly found himself hurried out of the prison and sent to the Luftwaffe interrogation centre. It is extraordinary that even after his ordeal and the lapse of six months since the crash he was still subjected to the full treatment by the Luftwaffe including the hot and cold cell routine. After a further period in a German hospital he was repatriated back to England in January 1945. After convalescence and discharge from the RAF he resumed his life, first in partnership with his father and, then on his own, in the family leather business.

For the rest of his life Jack never spoke of his experience or discussed it with his family, even his parents, until, in 1990 when I was visiting him we started to talk about the past. On a later visit, when I suggested that I might write an account of what he had undergone to lodge in museum archives he said that he would never want to see anything of the matter in print. For that reason I have abridged much of what passed between us.

The above account then has been written from memory after talking to Jack about his experiences over forty-five years after the events described. It would be impossible to put into words the full story of his imprisonment and I have really only attempted to outline the events in order to show that one member of our crew not only failed to receive the treatment he was entitled to as a prisoner of war but did not even receive basic humanitarian aid; as a result of which he suffered permanent disability. Even after all those years, during which he had barely spoken about the events described, it was obvious that the pain and suffering of those nine months remained vivid in his mind and therefore this story must be just an outline. One thing that did endure was the friendship formed at that time between Jack and the British paratrooper, both of whom lived in the same city of Nottingham and so were able to meet regularly over their lifetime.

Jack remained very active and, in spite of his disability, continued his business until he died in 1996 at the age of eighty-three.

Chapter X

Holland to Belgiun – A Close Call

To resume my own story. For three days I stayed hidden in the village of Slenaken including a visit and an overnight stay with Herman Ankoné in his flat in the village. Moving me around like a hot potato was obviously a sensible precaution in view of my later knowledge about the possible dangers of gossip.

Some aircrew in Bomber Command developed a habit of carrying a razor and soap with them on operations in case they had to bale out and it was, of course, also useful in the event of having to land away from base on return if the weather was bad or the aircraft had problems. On the whole it seemed to me to be a practice that appeared to tempt Providence and, since I did not consider being on the list to get the chop, my shaving kit stayed in its place back in my quarters at Holme. After four or five days without a shave I was beginning to look somewhat scruffy and after asking Sergeant Vermeulen for the necessary I was supplied with brush and soap together with a rather wicked-looking cut-throat razor. I repaired to the bathroom to get to work. Up to this time my only training in the use of such a weapon was occasionally watching barbers ply their trade. I drew upon all my past memories and got down to the business of removing the stubble covering my face. The result made me look like a victim of Dracula and certainly showed more injuries than I had received so far from the enemy. Vermeulen took one look and the next day produced a safety razor.

It was during these three days with the Dutch police that I was given a form to complete with which I was not very happy. Admittedly it was not headed 'Red Cross' but the amount of information required was on the same scale as the form which we had been constantly warned the Luftwaffe were likely to present to aircrew during interrogation. I demurred, but was told that a check had to be made to ensure my bona-fides and that the answers on the form would be radioed to London. I reckoned they had taken me on trust and therefore I had to reciprocate. At least London would know of my whereabouts and who was the missing survivor. I assumed, also, that London would advise my family that I was still alive, but that proved to be a forlorn hope.

Arrangements by now had been made for me to start on my journey to Spain and my French 'Carte d'Identité' was all prepared using one of the escape photos. An admirable forgery, it needed but my thumb prints, with the assistance of the Dutch police, to make it as good as the genuine article. Indeed, the cards were the real things: it was only the information and certifying signatures which were false. Years later I learnt that a reserve of these French and Belgian cards was kept hidden under the stones in the porch of the church in Teuven that I had observed in my first days in occupied Europe.

I was to leave Slenaken on the Sunday evening to go down into Belgium, although, at the moment, I still had no Belgian identity card. This, it was understood, would catch up with me. Late that night, with my police friends, I left the village and was handed over to a guide who was to escort me to the first stop in Belgium. It was a fairly quiet journey as we walked for a couple of hours or so, through woods mainly, and along country paths in the black of the night and, once or twice, stopped as the guide reconnoitered to make sure all was clear ahead. Although he had some English we walked in silence and any necessary talk was conducted sotto-voce since, in the silence, voices carried a considerable way. Eventually, we arrived at a Belgian farmhouse where I was delivered to my new hosts, a farmer and his wife, with the information that the stay would be limited to one night and I would be collected on the following day, Monday 1st May. Following coffee I was taken upstairs to an attic

room and with an injunction not to be seen at the window was left
to sleep till the next day.

From 'The Escape' in Holland I had now been passed to 'L'Armée
Secrète', a London-run organisation operating in the east of Belgium.
It was one of several organisations such as 'Comète' and 'Broken
Wings' which operated in Belgium to get aircrew and others out of
the country. But, in any case, these were code names of which I knew
nothing at the time.

Monday morning came and breakfast was brought up to the attic.
Since the toilet was outside the house normal personal needs were
met by the use of a bucket as it was usual practice within the escape
lines that evaders were kept out of sight except when on the move.
During the course of the day no one appeared to collect me and it
was obvious from the worried couple that this was unexpected and
something had happened to cause the delay. Lunch and evening meal
passed before instructions came that another night would have to be
spent there and hopefully there would be more information in the
morning. After a night's sleep, followed by breakfast, word arrived
that the move was to be made after lunch. No explanation was given
for the delay and, indeed, I did not expect to be given one, but in the
event it gave me that luck which all successful escapers and evaders
needed, and I did have my fair share. (The reason for the hold-up,
which I only learnt in 1978, was that a British officer involved in
L'Armée Secrète had been arrested by the Gestapo and this had
caused some confusion within the organisation. The particular
officer disappeared and was presumably executed.)

After lunch in mid-afternoon I was taken outside the house and
introduced to a bicycle which was to be the mode of transport. We
cycled for a few minutes until we were out of sight of the farm and
then dismounted to wait by a gate on a country lane. Almost
immediately, we were joined by a mother and daughter with whom
I was to spend the next seven weeks although this was not realised
or even expected at this moment. Both of them were mounted on
cycles and it was explained to me that Madame Coomans would

lead the way, Mady the daughter, would follow at a distance of fifty metres, while I was to follow keeping the same distance behind Mady. In the event of Madame being stopped or running into any problem, Mady would turn around, which would indicate that I should do the same: I would then be overtaken by Mady who would lead me off the road until things settled down. Without more ado, I bid my farmer friend and his wife adieu and we set off in line astern at fifty metre intervals.

Of this particular journey I remember very little of the route taken, except that we kept to open country. With the vision defect, which was still causing problems, I could only stare ahead as any turn of my head to right or left gave instant blurring of vision which, on a bike, also gave some balance difficulty. How long we cycled, again, I have no memory, but eventually in the early evening we came to the outskirts of what appeared to be a large village (in fact, the small mining town of Wandré) and entered the gates of a walled house where we parked our cycles in an outhouse. Madame Coomans hurried me to the front door of the house where we were met by the parish priest whose home it was. The curé of Wandré was a handsome man, probably in his late fifties at this time, and he led us into his dining room to sit down to a very welcome meal. He had a limited knowledge of English but in our conversations he made it quite plain that his loyalties were first to Belgium, with the church second. As time went on with my stay in this area it became obvious that while the curé may not have been physically involved in resistance activity, he certainly was aware of all that was happening and acted as a filter and link between different groups.

Shortly after 9:00 p.m. when it was quite dark we parted from the priest, Reverend G. Houyet, and made our way along the deserted main road of Wandré to Madame Coomans' home to begin what was to prove a remarkable seven weeks of evasion, not just from the enemy but also from Madame's husband. Her house was set back some thirty feet from the road with others which were fed by a roadway running parallel with the main street of Wandré. It was about 9:30 in the evening when we arrived and sat round the table to drink coffee, ersatz, naturally. At this stage I had no French, Madame and Mady no English, so the conversation was somewhat limited and often confined to single words at a time, laboriously researched from a French-English dictionary. We had entered the house by the side-door into the kitchen-scullery, through which we passed to the living room. This was the main room, probably measuring some fifteen by twelve feet, with the front door leading directly onto the street we had just left. A dining table was central to the room, with a bed-settee against the front wall under the window, a fireplace opposite to the door from the scullery and there were two other doors on the back wall. One of these went down into a cellar and the other directly opened on to the stairs leading to the bedrooms.

Now there was the opportunity to study my new friends and guardians. Madame Coomans stood only around five feet two inches and in repose had a rather doleful expression which belied, what later became evident, her acute sense of humour. She was very slightly built and moved lightly on her feet. It later became clear that she would have protected me to the death. Mady, taller than her mother by a couple of inches was of a more stocky build and very much in the Girl Guide mould; she was indeed a guide leader.

At 10:15 Madame led the way upstairs. The stairway proved to lead directly into a bedroom above the living room and a doorway to the right opened directly from this into a second bedroom. I was taken through into the second bedroom where there was a comfortable double bed. It was made plain that I was to stay extremely quiet and Madame would bring me breakfast at about 10:15 the next morning; until when, I was to stay in bed. Before I had begun to undress we heard footsteps on the main road turning off into our loop road. With a last enjoinder to stay quiet she left to go downstairs turning the key in the lock and taking it with her. Hurriedly undressing, as I heard M. Coomans enter the house, I crept into the bed and, then on, for the rest of the night, attempted to emulate the proverbial mouse; fortunately at that time of life no one had ever accused me of snoring.

That first night with the Coomans I slept in fits and starts, trying to come to terms with the cat and mouse game being played away from the security of England. Madame Coomans' husband had come up to bed about half an hour after I had settled in and I listened as he undressed, got into bed, and in a very short time was snoring his head off. It seemed to me that since I could hear his movements it should not be beyond reason that he might be aware of a presence the other side of the door at the foot of his bed. Every move I made in the bed seemed to produce a squeak or creak which, to my ear, was amplified a hundredfold; and any tendency to cough had to be rigorously suppressed, as did the need to blow my nose. It is sometimes difficult, in retrospect, to recall that first night, for, over the next seven weeks it became such a normal routine to sleep in this situation that it ceased to hold any qualms. Yet always, I had to stay aware of the need to stay quiet.

Morning came and some time after 8:00 a.m. M. Coomans could be heard to stir, climb out of bed, dress, and then make his way downstairs. Waiting for breakfast, I began to take stock of my surroundings. The room had two windows, one fronting on to the road and the other on the scullery side of the house; both were shuttered as, I was to find out, were all the other windows, up and down. Some light came in through cracks in the shutters which gave a subdued daylight throughout, sufficient to be able to creep out of bed and wash from a jug and bowl standing on a table by the wall. I had been given a safety razor and shaving brush by the Dutch before I left Holland and now quietly shaved as voices drifted up from below. Feeling more presentable I crept back to bed and awaited events. At around 10:15 a downstairs door slammed followed by footsteps along the road and a few minutes later the door was unlocked as Madame appeared with breakfast on a tray. As I ate she sat on the bed and we again attempted to converse but with very great difficulty. It appeared that M. Coomans would be back at 12:30 and I must stay confined to the bedroom. Apparently, once he had eaten breakfast, it was normal for him to make his way to the local estaminet to play cards with his friends. Meanwhile I got dressed.

Shortly after 12:30, we heard footsteps again which were quite distinctive and were becoming recognisable to my ear, so the bedroom door was re-locked and as M. Coomans entered downstairs I resumed my place on the bed and awaited the next move. This came at 1:25 when M. Coomans left the house for the local coal mine where he worked on a permanent 2-10 shift and so set my routine for the next seven weeks. After his departure I was free to go downstairs and relax until his return at 10:25 p.m., at which time, hearing his footsteps, we would hurriedly make for the bedroom where I was again locked in to face the same routine for the next twenty-four hours. Several times during the next few weeks I asked Madame Coomans, the curé, and another visitor what would happen if her husband found me in the house. Always the conversation was the same. "He would tell you to leave." "But would he not tell the Germans?" "No, I don't think so." "Then why would he not let me stay?" "Well, he is neither for the Germans nor against the Germans. He is neither for the English nor against the English. He's a miner. He would simply want you to go." Somehow, I never felt really assured by such a simplistic answer.

The first afternoon, after lunch had been consumed, the curé called and it was made plain that if at any time it became necessary to leave the Coomans' house I was to make my way to his home. To this end, it was explained, that in the event of a search of the area I was to vacate the house through the side window in the bedroom, on to the roof of the outside toilet and away up the wooded slope at the back whence it was possible to walk round the edge of the town to the curé's house. At the time it seemed a nice simple plan but later events were to prove it to be impracticable.

Time, initially, hung very heavy as ways were sought to pass the hours. Mady, the daughter, who was also twenty-one, was out for most of the day, presumably working. Madame often left me alone during the afternoon to go shopping on the black market and, in her absence, I was bidden not to make any noise in case it attracted the attention of neighbours. A dictionary helped to pass the time and to build up a vocabulary of French: always in reserve was the radio by which knowledge of the outside world could be maintained with the services of the BBC. A couple of days or so after my arrival in Wandré a lady visited me who would have provided my next port of call in the escape line. She had had two other RAF aircrew in her flat in Liège awaiting my arrival but due to the one-day delay in collecting me they had gone on in what proved to be the last run from the L'Armée Secrète line, via the Comète line to Spain. My new friend apologised at not having been able to wait on my arrival since a timetable had to be adhered to: nevertheless one felt a bit sick at having missed the boat, particularly as no explanation had been given for the delay. A week later I was able to thank my lucky star when the news was brought that the Liège lady would not be seeing me for a couple of weeks due to the necessity to vacate her flat and go into hiding in case the Gestapo were on her track. Apparently her two aircrew had joined up as planned with others and had been taken through Brussels down into France. It was unfortunate that mixed in with the group of ten or so was a German plant posing as an evader who, waiting until he had got as much information as possible about people and places, gave the signal somewhere around Paris and the whole group was picked up by the Germans. Immediately the enemy started raiding any houses on which they had gleaned information through talk among the aircrew. Fortunately the two from Liège had kept their mouths shut on the journey and after two weeks without any contact from the Gestapo my Liège lady felt it safe to resume her normal life. Had I been collected on time I would have been put into the bag with the rest of the group.

On her return from hiding, the Liège contact, who spoke good English, visited me again and was able to supply me with a number of English books together with a French equivalent of Hugo's language books, which while written in French to learn English proved very useful in overcoming the language barrier.

Two or three times during the seven weeks I was with Madame Coomans a man appeared who seemed to be the paymaster for the organisation since he always enquired about the state of my shoes and clothing and made some sort of subsistence payment for me to Madame. As I was confined to the house it was obvious that my shoes were not suffering any wear and likewise the only part of my clothing getting any use was the seat of my pants due to all the sitting around. Hence, there was no demand on my part for clothing.

Time drifted on into weeks and it became clear that there would be no further opportunities to get down to Spain and home. Although I did not know about it at the time, London had ordered the closure of all the escape lines because, due to the bombing of the railways in France, it had become too dangerous to travel. The daily routine was sometimes broken by a visitor, that is, the curé or one of the other two members of the line already mentioned. Sundays were slightly different, as while M. Coomans did not go to work he did tend to be out of the house for much of the time. It always seemed that he accepted the locked door leading from his bedroom although there was one morning when after getting up he came to the door and tried the lock. There was a loft in the house, the entrance to which was about halfway between my door and the head of the stairs in the main bedroom. On two Sundays when M. Coomans had left the house his wife produced steps and I took up residence for a few hours in the loft until he had returned to find the second bedroom door opened with everything within in apple pie order, and, of course, empty.

At one point the curé came along to ask whether I would like to take an opportunity to go to Switzerland but although freedom from the confined life I was leading seemed to have an attraction, on balance, the thought of perhaps being interned in that country until the end of the war was something that had little appeal.

Within two or three days of arrival in Wandré my French identity card had been supplemented by a Belgian one together with an ausweis (work) certificate which indicated that I worked on the night shift (10:00 p.m. to 6:00 a.m.) at the local coal mines, but, of course in a sedentary occupation as a clerk. This was done with the intention to give good reason why I was not at work in the event of being stopped at a check point during the day. Obviously, although the papers were almost perfect forgeries, the blank papers themselves being the real thing, nevertheless they were only expected to get one through routine checks. In the east of Belgium, with their fairly recent memories of the First World War, the Belgians, when they realised the Germans were again over-running their country in 1940, went to their town halls and removed any documents or records which were likely to incriminate individuals, taking new identities for themselves where they considered it prudent. Hence the Gestapo did not take too much notice of papers in their round-ups, although anyone not carrying them would excite immediate suspicion. So I put my French and Belgian cards in different pockets of my jacket which was always with me, just in case I had to run.

Sometimes Mady would clear the table and we would play table-tennis which was enlivened by her Pekinese who sat in a basket by the fireplace and took unkindly to my feet encroaching on his space. This gave Mady a rather unfair advantage in that I had to be aware of what was going on both above and under the table. My recollection is that Mady won most of the games and it all became part of the routine of passing time. Cigarettes always were freely available although had I been aware at the time of the problem and cost in obtaining them on the black market I would probably have given up smoking then and there.

Came D-Day on June 6th and no sooner than M. Coomans had left the house Madame burst into my room with the news and for this special day I went downstairs to breakfast in order to listen to the radio. What excitement there was! Everyone knew that it was only a matter of time before freedom would once again return and, I for one, certainly did not envisage at that time that it would be three more long months before I would return home. A few days later, as a result of D-Day, Madame Coomans informed me that a gentleman would be calling to discuss whether I would join L'Armée Blanche. This would be a free choice and if I did not wish to see him she would tell him to go away: she was rather protective towards me and I suspected that I was fulfilling the role of the son she would have liked. It appeared to be rather churlish not to see the man and so he duly arrived.

His job, so I gathered, was to recruit and organize the White Army, which in the event of prolonged resistance by the Germans, would operate in the Ardennes to the south of Liège. To this end he was in touch with other Allied aircrew, some of whom were already living in the Ardennes, and at the appropriate time he would arrange for me to join them. First thoughts about this were not too favourable; aircrew was a specialist business which did not take crawling about in the forest with a .303 into its training schedule. Nevertheless, I was a volunteer at heart and never did learn not to stick my neck out, so it was agreed that in a last resort situation, if things got bad, he could call on me to join up in his band. He duly registered me on his list and departed. Would it have made any difference to the rest of the story if I had not seen him? I do not know. Certainly he had been pressing to see me for some time. Madame Coomans had resisted but, after further pressure, she finally left the decision in my hands, which almost proved our undoing.

* * *

Monday 19th June dawned and passed like most other days with no indication that it would be any different. Mady did not come home in the afternoon as she was visiting friends and at about 6:40 in the evening Madame left me in order to get extra food on the black market. The radio stood on a small table between the scullery and front doors and being near to the street it was always advisable to keep the volume as low as possible, particularly when listening to the BBC. I pulled a chair up close to the set and tuned in. Most people of that era will remember 'Monday Night at Eight' which, if memory serves aright, became 'Monday Night at Seven' during the war years. About twenty minutes after Madame had left the house the programme began with the familiar signature tune, "It's Monday night at seven o'clock, oh, can't you hear the time, it's telling you to take an easy chair, so settle by your fireside, pick up your Radio Times, for Monday night at Seven is on the air".

All seemed at peace as I listened to the first few minutes of the show. Suddenly there was the sound of squealing tyres, slamming car doors and heavy footsteps running. There was a crash on the door (two feet away from me), and shouting voices to 'open up'. It took a moment for the penny to drop: for, to someone brought up in England in those pre-war years the knock on the door was not a thing we were familiar with. Now the shouting and knocking was at the scullery door and also the shuttered windows. I switched off the radio, turned the dial away from the BBC station, and tore upstairs to get away through the bedroom window. But there was no shortage of Gestapo officers. As I reached the window to open it so one of them was on the outhouse roof outside battering at the shutters in order to get in. I was trapped!

During the seven weeks I had stayed in the house, although at times alone, I had never ventured into the cellar. Now, if only to put off the evil for a few moments longer I went like a scalded cat back down the stairs. Fortunately, they had still not broken in downstairs although I later understood that there were six of them altogether. I kept moving fast down the cellar stairs which were of solid concrete. It was dark with just a glimmer of daylight coming through a small grating. As my eyes adapted and I heard the smashing of windows upstairs it became obvious that I was still trapped. There was nowhere to hide and no escape. Apart from a few beer crates the cellar was empty. Heavy footsteps were pounding about upstairs and voices were shouting to each other. I went to the darkest corner by the steps and there my luck again was in. At the base of the concrete stairway was a cavity about three feet six inches high, twenty inches wide and, as it went the full width of the stairs, I had plenty of room to hide. I grabbed some beer crates, made two piles, crawled into my hole and pulled the crates tight against the stairway to cover up. Just in time! Two Gestapo officers came down and ferreted around. Fortunately it was midsummer and the evenings were light so they had no torches with them. I watched through the beer crates, hardly daring to breathe, as they struck matches and peered around, walking right up to the crates. My heart was thumping so loudly it seemed that they must hear it but, as I watched them through the crates as they came up close, to my relief, they decided that the bird must have flown and went back upstairs. After a further half-an-hour of talking and searching upstairs they at last left and silence once again fell over the house. What to do now? Had they left someone upstairs or, maybe, a watch on the outside of the house? The questions were unanswerable so I decided to stay in my hide and await the morrow.

Years later, I learnt that the White Army man had been taken by the Gestapo. Apparently, he had two mistresses, one of whom was of German extraction. He also had a bad habit of talking about his activities and so when he cast off the German mistress she was able to lay information against him. He was arrested and after torture, disappeared, the Gestapo first having obtained all they wanted to know including information about me contained in his records. The one thing they did not know was that I was an RAF officer. They had expected to find a Belgian on the run and, fortunately, had delayed their raid by twenty-four hours, which again gave me the luck I needed and enabled Madame and Mady to keep their freedom. Had they been in the house it is likely that we would all have been taken. What was inexplicable was that, although a Belgian police officer who worked at Gestapo HQ sent his wife to the curé asking him to warn Madame Coomans that the Gestapo would be raiding her house the following evening, the curé took no action. One could only surmise that he thought he was being set up and there were too many other people involved. Madame found this out at the end of the war and never forgave him for she could not accept any reason for him not warning her.

When the Gestapo raided the house she was in a shop nearby and a neighbour came in to warn her. Madame Coomans may have lacked inches in height, but her courage more than made up for this. She fled out of the shop and made for the house. Another neighbour grabbed her and pulled her into his house. "You cannot go home, the Gestapo are in your house." Her reply was simple, "I must go to Thomas, he will think I have betrayed him." Her thought was not for her own safety, only that I should know that she had not deliberately left me alone to be taken by the Gestapo. She had to be physically restrained to prevent her from leaving her neighbour's house. She was a true Belgian whose pride could not be ground down by the invader. For three years or more she had sheltered people on the run, including two RAF aircrew earlier in the war, almost every night on their way to safety. All of them had stayed in the loft over her husband, in most cases for just one night, before they moved on. I was the last and only one to take over the bedroom because of the standstill order.

Back in my hidey-hole in the cellar I squatted as best I could and dozed the evening and night away. M. Coomans did not return at his usual time and I still suspected that the house might be watched. Between 5:00 and 6:00 in the morning I recognized M. Coomans' footsteps coming towards the house. He entered and after a short time went up to the bedroom. I later understood that he had been picked up on leaving work and taken to Gestapo HQ where he had been grilled through the night. He must have satisfied them of his neutrality, for they eventually released him but how he convinced them that living in a four roomed house he was not aware of a 'guest' I never could understand. Maybe, it was, after all, because he was a miner! On the following morning he went through his normal routine, getting up at the usual time, breakfasting, going out to meet his mates, coming back for a bite to eat before making off to work at 1:20. Normality had returned so I resolved to leave the house at 5:00 p.m. and make my way through the woods to the curé's house.

Time dragged along that afternoon, relieved only by the plentiful supply of beer in the cellar which, fortunately, was of a lower gravity than even the wartime beer back home. It was almost 4:00 p.m. when light footsteps which had a familiar ring could be heard pattering about in the house. I crept out of the cellar and then upstairs to the bedroom where Madame Coomans was at her dressing table collecting a few personal belongings. She was overjoyed to see me, for, while everyone knew the Gestapo had drawn a blank, my 'disappearance' had been a mystery. She and Mady were going into hiding but she would warn the curé to expect me sometime that evening. With that, she left and I waited until 6:00 p.m. before slipping out of the side door and up into the woods at the back of the house. An hour or so later a squad from the Luftwaffe, who had been advised by the Gestapo of my presence, arrived and again turned over the house presumably in an attempt to discover my identity. By luck, my timing was again impeccable.

After leaving the house and making for the woods on higher ground at the back I now had the task of finding a house which I had only seen once some seven weeks before in the dusk, and moreover, finding and entering it without being observed. Fortunately my sense of direction had always been good and although acting as a bomb aimer for the last year, I was still instinctively a navigator. In order to keep out of sight of the houses in the main street below, I went deeper into the woods and more or less made a crescent shaped route to the curé's house. Perhaps, more by good luck than judgment I arrived spot on in the lane by the boundary wall and slipping out of cover followed the wall round till the gate came into view. Knocking at the door, I was soon hustled into the house although it was obvious that the curé would have been happier had I waited till it was dark. Although I was unaware of the fact at the time, my transfer from L'Armée Secrète, a London-run SOE organisation, to a Resistance group was now almost complete.

The curé's housekeeper had prepared a good dinner and we sat down and did justice to her cooking and to a couple of bottles of accompanying wine. Over the meal we discussed the Gestapo raid and my narrow escape from capture but in no way did the curé give any hint that he had had prior knowledge of the raid. That information only came by chance to Madame Coomans some little time after Belgium had been liberated. In a detached way I could understand the curé's possible motives although I knew nothing of this until thirty-four years later so was unable to discuss the matter with him since he had, by this time, died: but Madame, to her dying day at eighty-nine years old, still had no forgiveness.

As dusk fell, we were joined by two men whom I was to come to know as Jacques and Jules. Jacques Gilles (real name Warnant) was a small, wiry man, some five feet five inches tall, while Jules was taller by perhaps three or four inches and of a heavier build. At a signal, I bid adieu to the curé and left his house with my two new guardian angels to seek security elsewhere in the town, or perhaps, to put the place in perspective, it would be better described as a mining village. There was really only one main street which ran parallel to the railway both more or less running on a north-south axis on the east bank of the River Meuse. We hurried through the deserted streets and eventually entered the back door of a small house straight into the kitchen where a group of four people were sitting awaiting my arrival.

A woman of about forty, somewhat to my surprise, addressed me in perfect English with a slight Black Country accent. Marie Warnant, alias Gilles, was the wife of Jacques and as far as I was aware was the only female member of this resistance group. She later explained to me how, as a child, during the Great War she was evacuated from Belgium and lived in the Midlands for the duration. Again the conversation quickly turned to my evasion of the Gestapo and the history of my stay so far in Belgium and Holland. Although, obviously, this was a committee to establish my bona-fides it was a different organisation from the escape line and while they knew of

Madame Coomans' involvement, I made no attempt to identify any other people or places other than where I had been shot down. The group appeared to be quite happy with my attitude on this matter. They themselves knew that as a group, they relied on as few people as possible having information. Indeed the security of the resistance groups was based on only two people in each group having contact with other groups, which ensured that should the Germans break one group it was unlikely that they would penetrate any others.

Eventually, it was time to move and I was taken in charge by a man of some sixty years with whom I was to stay for a few days until arrangements could be completed for me to stay in the country. We took our leave of the others and walked along a path between the line of houses and the railway and turned in to the back of the terrace house where my host lived. M. Poitevin was a widower, living alone, so there was plenty of room in the house and my bedroom was quite comfortable, so I slept well. In the morning I got up with M. Poitevin who made breakfast for me and then went off to work, leaving me to my own devices. His place of work was, in fact, not far away, being a small engineering factory at the end of the garden, adjoining the railway, which we had passed through.

For the next few days, I played an advanced game of hide and seek as I overcame the major snag of staying in this 'safe' house. The only toilet for the house was outside in the garden being about ten yards from the back door on the opposite side and fully in view of the upper windows of the house next door. My approach and retreat was therefore a major operation every time nature called since the family living in that dwelling were members of the Rexist Party, (Belgian Nazis), and the son was in the Waffen SS. A slight gap in the door enabled me to check whether I was being observed before stepping out to return to the cover of the fence and the back door: but getting to the toilet was slightly more hazardous since my back was to their windows and it was essential first to make sure the way was clear by cautiously peering up at the windows from behind the security of the fence before making a dash across the garden. Never before or since, I suspect, has anyone had such a sense of excitement from going to and from the loo!

Working close at hand, M. Poitevin was able to return at lunchtime and produce something to eat to see us through until he could make a main meal in the evening. Time passed rather slowly during the day but after clearing up in the evenings we engaged in conversation over a wide range of topics made necessary by my limited French which often brought a particular subject to a close when we ran out of understanding causing a switch to something else. Politics naturally arose and it was soon plain that my host and friends were very much of the Left, as were, indeed, many of the members of resistance groups who were looking to change the balance of power when liberation came. Fortunately, as I found out, politics were no bar to being a member of this particular group which accepted what each could contribute rather than their beliefs.

Two subjects continually came up and were to cause me minor embarrassment for the rest of my stay in Belgium. First, now that the invasion had been well and truly established for nearly three weeks, people came again and again to seek my views on how the attack would develop. Useless to protest that I was somewhat detached from ground operations having had no training in such matters; I was an RAF officer and as such I had the impression that I was expected to be au fait with the thoughts of Ike and Monty. Nothing that could be said seemed to dispel this illusion so by dint of very guarded and cryptic remarks based on the Ministry of Information posters in England, I eventually maintained the position expected of me without having to reveal my appalling ignorance of military strategy.

The other problem was really connected with the First World War. Everyone from that era had memories of 'Tipperary', 'Pack Up Your Troubles', 'M'moiselle from Armentières' and all the other famous marching songs of the British Army in that period. Now I was expected not only to be able to predict what songs the infantry would be singing this time but also to teach the words and music. Usually I found a little prevarication was sufficient to have the subject put aside; that is, until the next enquiry came along when I again went through the same routine of ducking the issue.

To come back to M. Poitevin; it was never intended that I should stay long with him since there were obviously difficulties in being left alone all day and Marie had said at our first meeting that I would be taken into the country in due course. At the end of June, word came that arrangements had now been made for my transfer out to a nearby farm. Jacques and Jules turned up to escort me again and I said my farewells to M. Poitevin. I think he was sorry to see me go for we had been good company for each other.

The three of us walked through Wandré in the late afternoon turning off at the lane passing the curé's house. We walked up the hill out of the village and I was struck by the different procedure that I was now undergoing in comparison with movement in the escape line. In the past I had been on my own following my escorts at a distance conforming to the instructions given. Their first objective had to be to maintain their organisation and, to that extent, individual aircrew and other evaders had to be expendable, and rightly so, since the lines had to stay in being. Now it seemed to be a different ball game. As we moved out into the country, I raised the matter with my escorts. In the event of being stopped did I isolate myself from them or what stance was to be adopted? It was quickly made plain that in the event of trouble, the first priority was my safety. They would deal with any problems, emphasizing this, as they patted the pistols in their waistbands.

A few minutes walk and we came to a small crossroads on which stood one or two buildings including an estaminet on the right hand corner. About thirty yards on across the junction on the left hand side stood a farmhouse which proved to be our objective. The front door faced onto the lane but we passed this, turning in behind the house into a courtyard formed by the house and barns and then entered the house through the scullery door where we were greeted by the smiling farmer. M. Schoofs was a tallish slim man with balding head and strikingly kind eyes. He introduced me to his family who I was to come to know so well over the next two months. Mme. Schoofs, his wife, a bonny buxom woman probably around forty, Pascal the son, eighteen, Andrée the eldest daughter, fourteen, and Jenny, eleven.

After a few minutes conversation my guides departed and I was left with the family and to take stock of my surroundings. Entry to the house had been through the scullery door from the courtyard and from there through to the main living room. This was a comfortable room running the width of the house with a large window facing on to the crossroads with a smaller window at the opposite end giving an outlook on to the courtyard. The room gave an impression of middle class comfort with a refectory table in front of the window with various pieces of other furniture and chairs around the room and an Aga type range against the wall on the scullery side. On the other wall were two doors, one at the table end leading into M. Schoofs' study and the one opposite the scullery entrance leading into the hall.

Madame Schoofs now introduced me to my quarters which were gained by a back stairway from the scullery. The room was small with a single bed and wash basin so that it was almost self contained. A small window overlooked the courtyard. Another door led to the landing from which I had access to a bath and toilet, a luxury long denied. After the last two months of close confinement the freedom to move about both in and out of the house was a luxury that took time to sink in. I had become conditioned to always being in a state of hiding but now I was almost expected to become part of the scenery and the first day after a good night's sleep was spent in adjusting to the new situation. Meals were taken at the large table by the window of the living room and visitors to the farm, including the postman, could not have been unaware of my presence. It seemed, after a while to be a more effective way to hide than being confined behind walls – and certainly more pleasant. No doubt, M. Schoofs was selective about who walked into the farmhouse but at the time there did not appear to be any obvious veto.

Twenty-four hours after my arrival an almost conspiratorial air was adopted by the family as it was explained that they were all going off for the evening except for Pascal. I gathered that I was to stay with him but my French was still not sufficient to understand in what nefarious enterprise I was to become engaged. In due course the family set off, presumably for an evening church service, and Pascal, after collecting a rather large knife, led me across to one of the barns. We entered and as he carefully shut the doors I became conscious that we were not alone. Tied up at one end of the barn was a young calf which was obviously the object of our visit. Apparently one of the Schoofs cows had calved and fortunately had produced twins. As in Britain all livestock births had to be declared to the authorities, in this case German, but in the event of twin births it was the norm to declare one and set the other aside to kill for personal consumption. It therefore had its danger as far as the Germans were concerned, hence the feeling of conspiracy I had experienced.

Pascal proceeded to find a cord and then led the animal into the middle of the barn before pulling it down to the floor. At this point he threw the cord to me to tie the calf's legs together while he continued to hold it down. This proved to be a big mistake since I had never been in the Boy Scouts and certainly lacked any experience in dealing with animals apart from milking a friendly goat occasionally when I stayed on a farm as a schoolboy. The 'tying' finished, we sat on the animal while Pascal reached for his knife and commenced to cut the calf's throat. The animal did not take kindly to this and in the ensuing struggle loosened the rope, regained its feet, slipped from our grasp and careered in circles round the barn with blood shooting in all directions. Judging by Pascal's language he was not very complimentary about my skill in knot tying but his outburst was rather brief as our main task was to regain the initiative and finish the job. This was eventually achieved without too much assistance from me and without getting covered in too much gore.

The calf was then hung up on one of the beams so that Pascal could proceed with skinning, eviscerating and cutting up the carcass which, incidentally, was going to give me many a good meal in the next few weeks. The whole operation must have gone according to plan and timing for shortly after we left the barn we were joined by the family who were obviously delighted that all had gone well.

Pascal recounted, to much laughter from the girls, my poor showing as a cowhand but although I felt somewhat abashed it was all done in good humour and I could not but join in the laughter, meantime, protesting that I was a Londoner not a country lad. So ended my induction into Belgian farming.

Chapter XI

Face to Face with the Germans

Time on the farm passed pleasantly with only very rare alarms occurring. The fruit season was just beginning and I soon established myself as a first class picker of soft fruits and then cherries and plums through to apples and pears later on in August. Early in September I was also to take a turn in scything hay and wheat fields but here my efforts did not seem to gain so much appreciation since I found myself relegated to the 'gathering' jobs.

During the period at the farm, food did not appear to be a problem and I probably ate better than in a wartime RAF mess. Certainly the fruit brought a delicious addition to the diet in the shape of open fruit tarts à la Belge, the taste of which has always lingered on my palate and remained with me. Once a week Madame Schoofs would have a baking day and would prepare flan cases of about eighteen inches diameter which would then be filled with fresh fruit. While this was going on the oven would be prepared. This was a large metal coffin-like structure with a door at one end and mounted on four legs which stood end on to the outside wall of the scullery. The oven was stone-lined and would be filled with brush wood which was then lit and allowed to burn through to ash before being raked out and replaced by the tarts. The results could only be described as superb.

Monsieur Schoofs was actually a cattle dealer but business must have been somewhat restricted by German controls for he seemed to spend more time on the farm than in the markets. Andrée and Jenny were both lively girls with a great deal of fun about them but, in retrospect, it must have been agony for their parents each day when they were at school wondering whether they would confide their secret to their friends. Strangely enough, life seemed so secure during this time that such a thought never occurred to me. The weather was good and I could wander in and out of the fields at will, play with the dog, pick fruit or simply sit and talk with callers.

Callers there were in plenty. Apart from one or two members of the resistance group, there were often folk from the farming community discussing problems with M. Schoofs and, of course, the postman who always delivered right into the living room and often enjoyed a cup of coffee if one was going. Probably there were up to twenty-five people outside of the family who knew of my existence at the farm and I well remembered one old boy sitting down with me turning to Madame Schoofs and, nodding in my direction, remarking that with the number of people who knew about me he would not be in her shoes for all the tea in China, or equivalent words.

This same farmer insisted one evening on offering me his tobacco pouch to roll a cigarette. There were times when packets of cigarettes did not come to hand when I then had to resort to rolling my own. This was one such time and, seeing me do this, my companion persuaded me to try his tobacco. There seemed little difference in the taste, much tobacco being home grown and cured on the Continent, but I was taken aback when he told me that he produced his own tobacco from cherry tree leaves.

Marie used to call at least once a week and would amuse me with tales of Jacques' nefarious activities and indeed her own. Many a time she would be collecting plastic explosive from Liège, carried in her shopping basket, and chatting with German officers as she walked through the town. In Wandré there was a level crossing on the railway line which carried supplies from France and Belgium through to Germany. It was not unknown for the crossing to be closed 'by arrangement' when goods in short supply were being transported. Immediately the train stopped a swarm of the local inhabitants would appear from the sides of the track, open the truck

doors, take their fill of potatoes, produce or coal and be away before
the German railway patrols knew what was happening. Marie was a
bit slow one day on a coal train and was the only one left when a
German guard caught her with a large bag of coal which she was
dragging away. Apparently she looked such a mess with black all
over her face that he cracked a joke about her appearance and let her
go, much to her relief. She told me that this sort of thing was going
on all along the lines and she often wished she could see the
Germans' faces when the looted trains arrived at their destination in
Germany.

Jacques, Marie's husband, worked locally in the electricity supply
industry. Two or three times a week he would be out for most of the
night following his chosen calling – blowing up electricity pylons with
the explosive brought by Marie. After such a broken night's sleep he
would be late in to work the following morning which to all intent
and purpose did not provoke any action from his boss who obviously
knew what was going on. Upon arrival at work Jacques would often
be sent out to reinstate the pylons and lines he had blown up the night
before – almost employment in perpetuity! Perhaps one could see this
as the solution for modern unemployment problems.

In the middle of July came a scare. One of the members of the
group had been picked up by the Gestapo and was held at their
headquarters. It was not known why he had been arrested but there
was an inevitable fear that he could talk if they were on to his
resistance activities. The Gestapo, in some ways, were very
predictable in that, when raiding premises to pick up suspects, they
invariably called early in the morning just before breakfast time or
early in the evening when people were home from work and settling
down for the night. For the next week therefore I was supplied with
an alarm clock and had to get up at 5:00 a.m., tidy up my room and
go down to a small wood at the end of the field there to wait until
about 8:30 when I could return to the house for breakfast. From
about 6:00 to 8:30 in the evening, it was again necessary to hide out
in the same place.

After a week of this it was obviously becoming a strain on the family and the decision was taken that I should go back to Wandré for a few days to stay with M. Poitevin until the trouble had blown over. In the evening the usual armed escort of Jacques and Jules arrived and we made the short journey back to Wandré where I settled down quickly into the old routine with M. Poitevin.

The resistance group received a lot of help with its finance from a wealthy scrap metal dealer, whose house and yard backed on to the railway several hundred yards along the line from where I was staying, and he had expressed a wish for me to dine with him. Accordingly, arrangements were made for Marie to collect and escort me along to his house. The route was to be out of M. Poitevin's back gate on to the railway line and along by direct means to the dealer's house. The railway was patrolled twenty-four hours a day by German troops who had been doubled up since the invasion in June. Within a few days of the doubling-up, the Resistance, presumably as a gesture, blew the line up in three places in the six or seven kilometres between Wandré and Liège. The German patrols were therefore on the qui vive.

We left the house and walked single file in the shelter of the fence to avoid any prying eyes from the Rexist neighbour, through the engineering workshop at the bottom of the garden, and thence on to the railway line. Jacques was on the line, where presumably he had been observing the patrols, and he gave us the all-clear to proceed before disappearing in the opposite direction. Marie led the way along the line which was in a shallow cutting so that we were out of sight of any houses, which were cut off by a continual fence. Our turn-off point was easily identified by a mountainous pile of scrap aluminium and we skirted this to arrive through a small garden at the side French windows of the house.

After introductions, we sat down in the large living room and were offered aperitifs while we chatted and got to know each other. A delicious five-course meal followed with a different bottle to accompany each course, the two ladies having a glass each while my host and I finished off each bottle. A bottle of cognac finished the evening but certainly we did not attempt to finish that off. It was now getting on for 10:00 p.m. and curfew, time to return to M. Poitevin along the railway line. Marie and I said our adieux to Monsieur and Madame Scrap-metal Dealer and slipped out into the gathering dusk back on the track. During the meal Marie had continually protested that she didn't normally drink but nevertheless did take a glass as each bottle came up. Now it became obvious that she really had meant what she said, for, as the night air hit her, she began to sway somewhat as we stepped from sleeper to sleeper and so I, perforce, had to become the guide. It became somewhat more alarming as her voice became louder and she began to get what one might call schoolgirl giggles which in the still night sounded as through they were a bugle-call to any German patrols in the vicinity. I drew the line at running up and down the bank singing Belgian nursery rhymes and managed to persuade her to keep going in the right direction. It was a relief when Jacques suddenly materialised out of the shadows and hurried us away out of danger.

It is peculiar in the way memory works how a single thing of very minor importance can be retained while everything else gets lost. Memories of sitting down with M. Poitevin at the table in the living room remains quite vivid but of the meals he prepared only one thing remains. One day he brought a lump of cold cooked meat to the table which looked rather like pink marble and, as he proceeded to slice it, I asked what it was. We had to resort to a dictionary but it was finally identified as cow's udder. Although I had a vague idea that somewhere in the north of England this was eaten, it was not something with which I was familiar but although I found the thought of eating it somewhat distasteful, nevertheless, it proved to be quite pleasant, and anyway, if it was good enough for my host then it had to be good enough for me.

Somewhere nearby was a member of aircrew who was suspect and, as once before, when I was with L'Armée Secrète I was on standby for two or three days to be taken along to see whether I could establish the individual as genuine or a German plant. In the former case my services had not been necessary since the escape line had been able to establish their case as genuine. In this instance, again, I was not called upon as, apparently, whoever had care of this 'evader' were satisfied as to his identity and he had, as I was told, been 'looked after'. Being in German Intelligence was not always a safe job!

After a few days with M. Poitevin, word came that it was safe to resume living with the Schoofs as the Gestapo had released the group member they had in custody. It seemed that his arrest had had no direct bearing on his activities with the group and I could now get back to the freedom of farm life.

As July turned to August it was almost frustrating to lie in the fields and look up at the tiny specks in the sky which were Forts and Liberators often only identifiable by the contrails. Occasionally, there would be a burst of cannon fire but on the whole they seemed to pass over this area unmolested by fighters but there were batteries of AA guns within a few kilometres and these would blaze away whenever the aircraft were in range. Generally, watching them was a link with England to reach out to, but it was very much a question of so near and yet so far. Now and again the Eighth Air Force would attack railway marshalling yards in the vicinity and the air would be rent with the scream of a large number of bombs dropping simultaneously followed by the ground literally shaking as the explosions took place.

I was again given the opportunity to go on a run to Switzerland but, as previously, when the offer came up during my time with L'Armée Secrète, the idea of being interned did not appeal and I made it plain that the only direction of interest was towards Normandy and home.

Now came a peculiar chapter in this saga for which I was never able to find a satisfactory explanation. Marie, on one of her visits to the farm and after talking to M. Schoofs for a few minutes, turned to me and asked if I would like to take a chance to get back to

England. It transpired that some other body had approached them to ask whether I would like to join up with an RAF pilot, the idea being for the two of us to hi-jack an aircraft from a nearby German airfield and fly back to England. After over three months of inactivity, I was ready to try anything once so agreed to give it a whirl. Marie admitted that they did not know anything about the people from whom the invitation had come but before they committed me they would wish to be satisfied that everything was above board and would be making the necessary enquiries. Three days after this conversation, word came that the group were satisfied that it was not a trick and that I should be ready to go in the afternoon.

It was a Sunday and I was once again escorted from the farm by the two J's, this time ending up at the curé's house again. The curé gave me an assurance that all the checks had been carried out and he was satisfied that everything was genuine and he hoped that all would go well so that I would shortly be back home. We agreed a coded message to be sent on the BBC in the event of being able to make it, before we were joined by a smartly dressed man, speaking very good English, who was to be my guide.

It was a very pleasant Sunday summer afternoon as we journeyed down to the main road and then boarded a tram to the centre of Liège. My companion warned me to be prepared to produce my identity card and work permit in the event of being stopped for spot checks. The tram journey of just a few kilometres was uneventful and we disembarked by the bank of the Meuse in Liège. Being a Sunday there was not much activity, although plenty of people, and we strolled along to one of the bridges to cross over. All bridges, as a matter of course, were guarded by German troops at each end and this one was no exception. Sometimes these guards would stop people at random to check papers but today they seemed somewhat lethargic brought about, no doubt, by the warm sunny weather. Reaching the west side of the river we crossed a large square and negotiated several streets before entering a large fashionable looking building which was separated into apartments.

During our journey from Wandré I had broached the subject of the proposed hi-jack of a German aircraft several times but did not seem to be able to get any positive response from my guide. Each time the subject was raised he somehow changed the line of conversation without giving any positive or negative indication of his knowledge of the plan. At this stage it did not seem untoward that my guide should not have such information so I did not press the matter.

Entering the block of apartments and mounting a broad staircase, we went into a large well-furnished room and were greeted by a group of three people, two women and one man. Now it was time for surprises. One of the women was Madame Coomans. We greeted each other warmly and then discussed past events. Mady had apparently gone into hiding in a convent, arranged probably by the curé of Wandré. Madame said that she had not been enamoured by the habit she had been forced to wear but when the hue and cry had died down and she could resume living with friends she became most indignant when she was decked out by the nuns in the most unfashionable garb one could imagine rather than her own clothes which had, apparently, disappeared. It was an indignity that was to remain with her for the rest of her life.

As we sat around the room drinking coffee I asked when the attempt was to be made to take the German plane and when was a meeting to be arranged with the pilot who was to do the flying. The questions met with a blank so I had to explain the reason I had come. Everyone in the room expressed ignorance of the plan but undertook to make enquiries and let me know if it was possible. In the meantime, arrangements had been made for me to stay in a safe house in Liège where it was hoped I would be comfortable.

My guide and I then left the apartment and made our way to a large square where we boarded a tram for a short journey through the city. Not having been out and about too much during my three month stay in Belgium I still had a slight feeling of unease in public almost as if a placard was hung round my neck reading "Je suis Anglais". No doubt many other aircrew in similar situations felt the same and somehow had to ignore this feeling and act for all the world in, as far as one could judge, a normal way. Nevertheless, this state of thinking did tend to keep the mind alert to what was going on and, I am sure, enabled one to react rapidly to any change in the situation.

As I walked through Liège with my guide on this August Sunday little did I know that I was only a stone's throw from Jim Lewis hiding in the cathedral, particularly with the assumption made that he was the unidentified body mentioned in the original German communiqué. After a few minutes we came to a long street and entered one of the buildings. Climbing three flights of stairs we knocked at the door of the flat and were greeted by an elderly couple. Introductions were made and we chatted for a while before Bertie, my guide, got up to make his departure. I again raised the matter of the attempt to steal a German aircraft but it became plain that he knew nothing of this and was somewhat embarrassed by my persistent questioning. He promised to get an answer on this by the following Thursday when he would call in to visit. With that, he went on his way and I was left with my new hosts.

Time passed slowly and after the freedom of the country, being cooped up in the middle of a city was extremely irksome, particularly, as I now suspected that the curé had been hoaxed in order to get me back under the wing of the escape line. In retrospect, it may have been a ploy devised by the curé himself, for whatever reason, to transfer me to Liège. Each day was like an age since I could only remain in the flat and listen to the sounds on the street below, at all times, of course, staying away from the windows. My hosts were very obviously nervous. It was probable that I was the first airman they had taken in and their concern rose as we heard almost daily German street searches going on in the surrounding area. My presence also produced a problem which had possibly not been quite so visible back in Wandré. Food was not as plentiful as in the country and while I was fed adequately, there was less variety in the diet. During my stay in Belgium I was always conscious of the embarrassment of my hosts at not being able to serve a meal to do justice to their culinary skills.

When Bertie dropped in the following Thursday, as arranged, he was unable to give any satisfactory explanation about the ruse that had brought me to Liège. Although I did not know at the time, Bertie was Madame Coomans' brother and, although he was not in L'Armée Secrète, gave the impression that he had some role in British Intelligence, He had had nothing to do with the arrangements for me to leave the Schoofs' farm although he had picked me up to bring me to Liège because he understood that I was not receiving adequate food and was in some danger.

Many years later Madame Coomans gave the same explanation so it became impossible to unravel the reasons why I was taken to Liège. One can only see this as confirmation of the mistrust which existed between escape lines which were non-militant and the active resistance groups, the leadership of which were often politically motivated from the Left wing. The escape line organisations did not like to see evaders pass from their control into the hands of the resistance, for what reason it is difficult to fathom. Perhaps they considered that there was more risk of the evader being captured and then made to talk with the possibility of betraying helpers in the escape line. From my own experience this seemed to be an injustice to resistance groups in general as I felt freer and yet safer with the group I was with than hidden away in the escape line. The people in the group seemed to be of varying points of view come together with a common purpose and with the end of the war they went their own separate ways. Maybe, I could only see the differences between the organisations from a very parochial point of view as it affected me, without understanding national politics which undoubtedly impinged upon this whole matter.

For a few more days I stayed in Liège but the activity of the Germans in the town was becoming more and more intense. The sound of the Gestapo with their Belgian police collaborators roaming the streets below with horns blaring as they sealed off roads and raided houses was really beginning to cause distress to my aged hosts. In the event of entry by the Gestapo my escape route was to be through a skylight out on to the roof after which it was to be pot luck in finding another skylight by which to return to ground level. I decided that I could no longer put these kind people at risk and asked them to send for Bertie. He arrived a couple of days later and I told him that I was extremely uncomfortable about the risk the couple were running and did not consider it right that people of their age should have to live in such fear caused by my presence. After some discussion, it seemed that Bertie had no alternative to offer so it was agreed that he would escort me back to Wandré and leave me in the centre near the curé's house where we had first met and it would then be up to me to find my way back to the Schoofs. Since I had not disclosed my destination nor had discussed names or places where I had been since the Gestapo raid, this seemed the best way to maintain as much security as possible for the Schoofs and other members of the group.

Bertie duly appeared with two bicycles the following day in the late afternoon and we set off through the town and out on to the Wandré road for the five or six kilometre journey. We were accompanied for about a mile by a German trooper with a rifle slung over his shoulder who was also cycling our way. First we passed him and he then responded by a spurt to pass us. It did not seem to be the time to engage in a cycle race so we just all settled down to going along together. We exchanged occasional glances and he was quite obviously in an inoffensive mood to the point of a half smile as we were levelling up. Eventually, to my relief, our paths diverged and we completed our journey to Wandré on our own.

On reaching the lane leading to the curé's house I dismounted and handed the bike to Bertie. He turned around and after a warm farewell respected my wishes by riding back in the direction from which we had come. I waited till he was out of sight and then walked up the hill in the direction of the Schoofs' farm. The road was quite deserted until reaching the estaminet on the crossroads just by the farm. Looking in through the open door one could see a few of the local inhabitants playing cards round a table, none of whom evinced any interest in the passing stranger. A further thirty yards or so and I reached the farm entrance. The family had probably seen me coming along the road for, as I crossed the courtyard, Madame Schoofs came to the door to greet me as I made some remark about bad pennies always turning up.

Explanations had to be given for my return and while my reception was warm, it was many years before it occurred to me that while I might be priding myself on relieving the old couple in Liège of my presence, in fact, I was merely transferring the risk to the family with the children's lives all before them. Perhaps, after all, I was only thinking of my own comfort. In retrospect it is easy to develop such thoughts but at the time I felt comfortable and secure with the Schoofs, always having the impression that there would be a way out of any difficulty we might encounter. It would not be long before time would prove that.

* * *

During that summer I often lay in the fields on fine days and watched the contrails of the Forts and Liberators as they flew overhead. Sometimes one heard and felt the whine and thud of bombs as they bombed nearby targets. At other times my thoughts were with Bomber Command as they disturbed my sleep at night, in order that I could wish them all a safe return. If only I could take wings and fly up to join them. But even if that was impossible, the sound of those engines was always welcome to maintain the hope of soon getting away to rejoin the battle.

Thirty-three years later I was to visit my Dutch helpers for the first time since 1944 and received an overwhelming welcome. When I protested that the thanks should be the other way around for the help given this was brushed aside with the remark "You (the RAF) kept our hopes alive for four long years. The sound of your engines night after night was the only sign that the battle was still going on and one day we would be free again." I suppose this was the feeling I was experiencing on the Schoofs' farm.

There was now more time on my hands since, being late August, there was little to do on the farm which was only a few acres. There was a small field of wheat to harvest and my first efforts with a scythe did not bring forth the plaudits of the crowd so I was relegated to making stooks from the cut wheat. Other than this there was periodic apple and pear picking from the orchard, amusing myself playing with the farm dog and chatting with various visitors. This last occupation was, as recounted earlier, a little hazardous because of my limited military knowledge in being able to predict what our generals would do next. With the very fluid situation after the Normandy break-out any prediction made was likely to be proved wrong within hours so I became even more adept in ducking questions.

Talking one afternoon with another farmer the topic had drifted away from the war to cars and the three-wheeler Morgan he had driven before Belgium had been invaded. We had met once or twice before but he had not previously sought to find out anything about my circumstances. Now he questioned whether I was looking forward to getting back to England and in so doing asked how long I had been evading. When he knew I had come down in April he mused that he had helped an RAF officer at that time who had hit a tree on landing and needed to rest up for a few days. "What was his name? Ah – he was a big chap, his name was, ah – Jeem, ah – Jeem," I interrupted with "Lewis?" "Oui, that was the name, Jeem Lewis. Did you know him?" After explanations of having been in the same aircraft and the German report of the unidentified body which I had presumed to be Jim I was overjoyed to know that he was alive. I thought also of Nell, his wife, who would probably by now have had the baby she was expecting when we last met a few days before we parted company with our aircraft. But what happened to Jim, and where was he now? My visitor went on to explain that during the last four years he had been regularly engaged in passing to and from

France clandestinely. Since early in the year, with the threat of invasion, he had found it impossible to cross the frontier and, therefore, when Jim had recovered and made known his intention to journey south and cross into France on his own, my companion attempted to dissuade him, but without success. Jim then went on his way, arranging a coded message to be broadcast on the BBC if he was successful. That message had since been received, so Jim had obviously made it back to England. It was terrific news and buoyed me up with hope that I would soon join him. By now, I had come to understand the depth of hatred which the Belgians had for the Germans. At first, as a Briton, I had been unable to reach down that deep, it was so alien to our ethos. But living with it in the area first invaded by Germany in 1914, with the earliest war cemetery nearby the farm, I had come to ally myself to it and was itching to get back into uniform and resume where I had left off.

In a state of euphoria as the news of the Allied advance came over the radio it seemed a mere formality to wait for liberation and a lift home. But in this last week of August the consequence of that advance brought a new danger, the retreating German army. Although the farm was a little off the main roads, nevertheless, two of the four cross roads on which it stood could be used as a route to Germany and with the ascendancy of the Allied air forces many of the Germans were travelling by the back roads. As a result, night and day the farm became the centre of retreating groups who rested on the sides of the roads and in particular took up temporary residence in the orchard on the opposite side of the road to the front door. Because of this added risk and the tendency of some German units such as the SS to take pot shots at younger men I was now confined to the house.

The large window facing the crossroads gave a wonderful panoramic view of all that was going on and I could sit and watch to my heart's content savouring this culmination of five years of war. Most of the troops could only be described as ragged. They had few weapons with very little transport other than the odd bicycle or a

French farm horse and cart. There appeared to be no officers, most of whom had been withdrawn on Hitler's personal order after the Normandy breakthrough, and indeed, it is doubtful if many of the troops knew where they were. For two or three days I watched an old boy who, in between drinks at the estaminet, would take up position on the crossroads and willingly give directions to the retreating troops on how to regain the Fatherland. What became obvious was that he had put the roads on a rota system and no group was ever directed along the same route as the preceding one. When a convoy of three lorries appeared he even turned them back along the road they had come, to hopefully send them towards the advancing Allies.

Another marvellous little cameo took place one day when Jacques was coming along to visit the farm. Both he and his wife, Marie, had always told me how, when the German army had invaded in 1940, all their vehicles, tanks and uniforms were in immaculate condition: as they said, you had to admire what a "belle armée" they had. Now, as he bounced past the troops lying on either side of the road, grinning all over his face, he was giving the Nazi salute and shouting, "Heil Hitler". How he missed being shot is a mystery, although there were probably no officers to give any orders and these troops were not of Waffen SS standard, anyway. He turned into the farm, came straight through to the living room, crossed towards me and still grinning jerked his hand towards the Germans and almost exultantly cried "belle armée, heh, belle armée!"

After two or three days of this shambles of a retreat, one or two officers started to appear who had been sent back by the German High Command, in order to regain some discipline and organisation. Each morning for three days one of them came to see M. Schoofs seeking agreement to set up a temporary HQ but this was refused each time by Schoofs, after some argument. On the third day the German returned and announced that he was commandeering part of the premises and there would be fifty troops billeted in the barns that night. An advance party would be arriving just after lunch. I suggested to M. Schoofs that it might be advisable for me to leave, but he would have none of it. I was to stay quiet; under no circumstances was I to talk. If there were any questions as to my presence I was a deaf and dumb mute from the Flemish part of Belgium who was staying with them. The theory was that in spite of four years of occupation very few Germans had learnt French and even those that had, spoke with a very strong accent. Even so, they might still detect my bad French and so it was better to stay silent.

The morning passed all too quickly and we sat down to lunch shortly after midday. Here again chance was to help me once more in getting out of a tight spot. The long refectory table was set across the main window looking out on the crossroads. Normally I always sat on the long side with my back to the window. Today, however, we were joined by the daily help and a farm worker which caused a change in the seating arrangements in order for eight to sit down. I found myself, whether by accident or design, at the end of the table with the window on my left and the study door behind me. This door opened into the living room and thus with my seat in the way could only swing about eight inches before coming to a stop. The family and guests took up three seats on each side of the table with M. Schoofs sitting at the other end. Everything seemed normal as Madame Schoofs brought the dishes to the table and we tucked in to a roast with a full range of vegetables.

Halfway through the meal two small German trucks were sighted turning toward the farm from the crossroads and almost immediately they had turned into the courtyard where we could see them through the window at that end of the room. Without more ado, everyone had shot up from the table and dashed from the room into the scullery, leaving me the sole occupant of the room with a table loaded with half-eaten meals. There seemed to be no point in allowing my dinner to go cold so I continued eating on my own while listening to the commotion at the back door as the Belgians were harassing the Germans and generally 'taking the mickey' out of their every move. Suddenly I became conscious of movement outside

the window on my left and turning my head I was eye to eye with
two German signallers laying a field telephone to the study behind
me. The sight of the food on the table seemed to mesmerize them and
they were near enough drooling as they stood staring at it with their
faces pressed against the window. I decided to ignore them and
continued to eat in a desultory kind of way playing with the peas as
though I was not fully in charge of my senses.

Suddenly the signallers left the window and became very
interested in the equipment they were carrying. A moment later the
reason became clear. The study door behind me opened and was
stopped by my chair as the German officer from the morning pushed
his head partly through the gap. I could see him out of the corner of
my eye over the right shoulder as he made enquiries about moving
some furniture. He must have been dropped off at the front door,
coming through the hall which led into the study, without the
Schoofs being aware of his presence. For better or worse I had to
stick to the deaf mute act, perhaps, adding a little bit of the simple-
ton to it. So I ignored him. Meanwhile, the officer repeated his
question in a slightly louder voice while I continued to remain deaf
and to eat and knock peas off the plate in order to chase them round
the table. Now the German began to be irate and, withdrawing his
head, gave the door a hard push which rapped the chair almost
pushing my face into the plate before me as he, pushing his head
through the gap, for the third time, shouted out his requirements in
a voice that brooked no denial. It seemed that four and a half
months of evasion were now to come to a halt, as there was no
doubt that this gentleman was going to insist on an answer, but, even
as I prevaricated further the German was stopped in his tracks by
Madame Schoofs who had been attracted by his voice. She now
stood in the centre of the living room and, hands on hips, began to
let fly. The gist of her remarks were to the effect that the German
army had commandeered part of the farm but that gave them no
right to intrude into her kitchen; she would not have dirty Boche
boots on an honest Belgian woman's kitchen floor: if he had any

manners he would have come to the door and knocked and if he knew what was good for him he would get back to the other side of the door where he belonged. With that, Madame walked towards him, told him if he wanted anything he should come through the hall, and, pushing him back into the study, shut and locked the door.

By now Monsieur Schoofs had joined us and, realising the risk of what could happen, it was decided that it would be better if he made arrangements for me to leave. In the meantime, I was told to finish my meal, lie low in my room upstairs and he would let me know as soon as arrangements were made for my departure. I went up to my room and put together my shaving gear and the other few things needed and a short time later Pascal came up and said that I must be ready to go shortly after two o'clock.

Bang on time, Pascal came up again to call me down but this time there was a grin on his face as he told me that there was a guide downstairs who would take me to a place of safety. Other than that, no other instructions or explanations were given. I came down to the scullery where everybody was standing by the door into the courtyard and blocking the view, with Madame Schoofs talking to someone standing just outside. Andrée and Jenny were beginning to giggle and, getting on either side of me, assisted me through the door. I was dressed in pin-striped trousers with black coat and looked every one of my twenty-one years of age as I was propelled through the door to be confronted by a very large and extremely gross and bulbous Belgian peasant woman of perhaps thirty-five years wearing a long black coat. There were up to six or seven Germans lying about within the courtyard while a child of two to three years old was playing, running around and between them. No explanation of my role had been given to me so I was a little surprised to have a pushchair shoved into my hands as the woman called out to the child, "Now get into the pram, or Papa won't push you". I must admit to being taken aback at my new-found fatherhood but this was not the time to debate the issue with those German eyes turned in curiosity towards this rather incongruous couple.

As I held the push chair while mum seated the child in it, I looked back at the Schoofs family and company packing the scullery doorway. There were suppressed smiles emanating from the adults but Andrée and Jenny could hardly control themselves and were giggling like mad. This turned into laughter as they all called out their "au revoirs" and I maintained my deaf mute role throwing grunts over my shoulder and waving my arms as I pushed the child across the small courtyard past the recumbent enemy. It was perhaps only about twenty steps to travel but it seemed like half a mile before we reached the road and turning left put the big barn between ourselves and the troops. Somehow the infectiousness of the girls' hilarity had communicated itself to me and once out of sight of the Germans I became doubled up with laughter and let go the pram which I must have propelled as I did so for it was careering away with my companion having to move faster than I thought she was capable in order to save the pram and child from colliding with the hedge.

We reached the farm and I was sat down with a cup of coffee in the living room and told that I would be collected later in the afternoon. The time dragged by slowly and eventually Jules turned up to take me back to Wandré to stay once more with M. Poitevin. Jules found another way to take us back to Wandré rather than pass by the Schoofs' farm which was beginning to crawl with Germans. The next day Marie came to report that instead of the fifty troops billeted on the farm that night there were in fact nearer two hundred which would certainly have proved rather dangerous had I stayed.

Chapter XII

'A Voice from the Dead!'

M. Poitevin was pleased to see me once more as I took up my quarters in the familiar bedroom. Now for the next few days we began to hear the sound of guns as the Americans came closer and then we knew liberation was near at hand when not only the thump of cannon but also the whine of shells overhead could be heard. On Sunday 10th September, Liège was liberated by an American armoured spearhead with such speed that the Germans evacuated the town without burning it to the ground as many of their officers had promised. I was eager now to get back to England as quickly as possible and asked Marie to find the nearest US troops and take me to them.

On the Monday we walked south from Wandré towards Liège and found the colonel of the tank regiment leading the spearhead, to whom I made myself known. I was accepted without too many formalities and given some American cigarettes, but when I asked if he could get me back to his headquarters he laughed and said that he didn't have a clue where his rear headquarters were since they had to stay mobile to keep up with him. However, his rear headquarters liaison officer would be joining him at six o'clock that evening and if I returned then, I would be able to go back with him. With that I had to be content since there were still odd pockets of German troops behind the tank column and it was safer to travel with an escort than try to make it alone. I went back to Wandré to say my farewells.

During that afternoon I toured the Wandré area visiting as many of my helpers and protectors as possible. In many ways it was sad to part since I had in four months come to identify with these people who were absolutely indomitable and would never allow the Germans to get them down. Now as I did the rounds, several, including Marie, re-introduced themselves with their real names, dropping the non-de-plumes under which they had been operating for four long years. Sadly, I was unable to thank and say farewell to Madame Coomans whom I was given to understand had not yet returned home and, although I could have found my way to her house, it was probably not the time to thank her husband for his hospitality!

My last call was to the Schoofs where I had spent so many happy, though at times fraught, hours during that summer of 1944. Before leaving I was taken to a hall to see the bodies of five Belgian youths of eighteen years or so who had been indiscriminately shot by a retreating SS unit. They lay in open coffins with appalling wounds caused by dum-dum bullets and I undertook to report the SS commander to the appropriate authorities.

5:30 p.m. saw me back with the American tank colonel and we stood around waiting for his liaison officer to arrive. After some of the peculiar tobacco I had smoked during the last four and a half months the pleasure of American cigarettes was something to savour. 6:00 p.m. came with no sign of the liaison officer and by now the tanks were beginning to start up ready to move off. It was agreed that it would be pointless to continue to wait since it was the job of the liaison officer to find the tank column, not the other way around, so I accepted the colonel's invitation to climb into the jeep alongside him as the column set off to liberate more of Belgium.

We pushed ahead at a slow rate with periods of stop-start as the tanks negotiated turns. The joy on the faces of the Belgians as we drove through the villages and the odd small town will always live in the memory of anyone who was taking part in the liberation. Towards dusk a couple of JU 88s came in to attack but got themselves shot down, by whom, nobody seemed to know. One or two of the aircrew were in grave danger of being lynched by the local inhabitants and had to be rescued before being handed over to a resistance group to hold as prisoners of war. The column now pulled off the road into a large field and billeted down for the night. I had my first taste of American rations, which were very enjoyable and a change from my fare for the last few months, before curling up in a blanket under the open skies, well, actually a Sherman tank.

Came the morning with still no sign of the colonel's rear headquarters liaison officer and when, in discussion, the colonel said he was heading for the German frontier I could not refrain from pointing out that I had spent nearly five months to avoid having to go there and it was not part of my plans now to go in that direction. However, I was persuaded that if I showed a little patience the liaison officer would eventually appear and I would make faster time in getting back home. We rumbled forward again and as the column passed through villages and another small town, I was conscious of being the subject of curiosity among the populace, being the only non-uniformed person in the liberating force. As such I seemed to be missing out on the hospitality (bottles of wine, cakes etc.) being thrust upon us so could only presume that I was being taken for a Belgian guide.

In talking to some of the American troops about their break out from Normandy there was fulsome praise for the RAF in respect of the bombing in the Falaise gap and in particular to the tank-busting capacity of our Typhoons. To quote one of their officers: "Some German tanks were in our way so we called for some air support but were somewhat disappointed to see that all we got were a couple of Typhoons. But, gee, when those boys got to work they just opened up those tanks like a couple of can-openers!"

When we stopped for lunch I had made up my mind that I would start heading back on my own if the liaison officer had not arrived before the column moved off again. Consequently, when this time arrived I thanked the colonel for his help and reluctantly said farewell.

As the tanks moved forward, I started to walk back the way we had come but then became conscious of a jeep racing up past me to the colonel's jeep near the head of the column. It stopped for a few moments before retracing its path to pull up in a cloud of dust by my side, with a very welcome, "Wanna lift back home, fella?" coming from the Yank sitting behind the steering wheel. Back to the colonel for a little while longer and then, at last, I was really on my way back home. The weather was beautiful and the scenery glorious along the Meuse valley as the driver headed back towards his headquarters. He seemed to spend most of his time playing hide and seek between the tank spearhead, the rear HQ and other units, all of which were continuously on the move, and, somehow, he had to find them. It was a tricky job since there were many small units of German troops outflanked by the rapid advance of the allied tanks who often made life a little difficult and so he had to be on his mettle all the time.

Early in the evening we reached a large American tented field hospital where I was to sleep overnight and here I was brought face to face with the reality of war as I was led through the very large marquees full of wounded troops, many of whom had serious injuries. I was not sorry the next morning, after an American breakfast, to climb aboard a truck headed for Paris.

The collection of aircrew showing up after the liberation of occupied territory seemed to be within the normal routine of the advancing troops and in due course I was delivered to the King George V Hotel in Paris. The main recollection of that stay was seeing and eating white bread again and after nearly five months it was surprising how much joy one could get from merely gazing on and then sinking one's teeth into a piece of crusty white loaf.

It was at this hotel that RAF evaders were brought together and, because of the need to get us through the system and back to the UK, no individual interrogation was carried out. Instead we were given sheets of paper and told to write down our experiences. Whether anyone ever took the trouble to read them the Lord only knows. I hope so, for included in my report was the name of the SS officer responsible for those young men's lives in Wandré.

That evening we went out to see the town and have a drink using the escape kit French currency which I had not touched since my landing, having given the Dutch guilders to the Slenaken police before leaving the Netherlands and the Belgian francs to Madame Coomans. It was hard to believe that such a short time had elapsed since the Germans had been occupying this city doing the same things as we were now doing. The Parisians seemed to take everything in their stride, only the customers had changed and that included the women touting for business among the new troops. I bought a small bottle of Chanel 5 to take home, had a drink or so and wandered back to the hotel. I collected my room key at the desk and moved towards the lift only to receive a whacking great thump on the back accompanied by "If it isn't Syd Wingham", Syd being my first name which I used then. The face of Jim Lewis loomed over me as I turned round and looked up. It was only a week or so ago that I had been told Jim was back home, so what was he doing here?

We retraced our steps back to the nearest bar to swap experiences and marvel at the chance that had brought us together in the heart of Paris five months after wishing each other luck in the nose of that burning Halifax. Jim had attempted to make his way south but, as already related, ended up at the Chateau Sinnich and then on to Liège.

And so, having baled out together, we joined up to come home. A Dakota aircraft of Transport Command brought us back from Orly airport to RAF Northolt where we landed on Friday, 16th September and were fitted out with battledress and other issues to once again make us feel part of the service. A quick medical followed to make sure what sort of condition we were in and a six week leave automatically granted to enable us, presumably, to regain our health. I was not aware that mine had suffered but no choice was given. An interview then took place to enable us to choose what we wanted to do after our leave. Uppermost in my thoughts was one last crack at the Germans to make some payment for the suffering they had inflicted on the occupied countries. The idea of staying on 'heavies' or instructing did not appeal so I elected to return to operations on Mosquitoes.

So it was now time to return home. Having completed details twice for the Underground to notify London of my whereabouts and also having been under the wing of the Air Ministry for the past forty-eight hours I naturally assumed that notification of my safety would have been sent to my family. It was too late for Jim to catch a train to Hereford so I suggested he stay with me overnight at my aunt's house in South Croydon. At Victoria I telephoned Croydon to announce our imminent arrival. A friend of my aunt answered who knew me well. Obviously the Air Ministry had taken no action for, after announcing myself twice, there was a stunned silence followed by "Good God, a voice from the dead!"

We arrived at my aunt's home in Croydon and had a difficult time fending off questions about our stay on the other side being under orders not to discuss our experiences since there was always the danger of the enemy recapturing areas where we had been and taking reprisals. The next morning Jim and I travelled by train to London where I saw him off from Paddington on his journey home to Ledbury. My six weeks' leave dragged by slowly and although I tried to get back earlier I had to serve my full term of leave, enduring the occasional V2 rocket in the London area. During this time Jim and I visited the relatives of our missing crew members, giving them as much information as we could.

Eventually, my posting for a navigator refresher course came through which took me to West Freugh near Stranraer where I almost had to make a voluntary exit from the aircraft I was in on one flight to force a staff pilot to change course. We had been flying for two hours above 10/10ths cloud on basic DR navigation without any reliable fixes and he then announced that he was going to descend through cloud, in spite of my insistence to turn due west for ten minutes to ensure that we broke cloud over the sea. He brushed aside my objections; he was very experienced in flying in the area and knew where we were so he was going down. I warned him that

I would bale out if he continued. He did, so I put on a parachute, went to the rear door and called to the wireless op to tell the pilot I was about to open the door. The pilot then asked me to reconnect my intercom and agreed that if I was serious he would turn on to a westerly course. I assured him I was serious, so after ten minutes we descended and came out of cloud over the sea with the hills just a mile behind us shrouded by the same clouds. I never did get any thanks for saving his life!

After the spell in Scotland and operational training at Upper Heyford I ended up on 105 PFF Squadron operating Oboe where I managed four more trips before the war came to its end in Europe. This included the last raid by Bomber Command on Germany which was all Mosquitoes, some hundred plus, and I can claim to be in one of the last four aircraft of the Command to bomb, dropping a 4,000 pounder on the Luftwaffe base at Eggebek near Kiel on 2nd May 1945, and the last 105 Squadron aircraft to land after operations in World War II. And so ended my war.

Appendix

Very little attention has ever been paid to the agony and suffering undergone by mothers and wives of missing service personnel. When an aircraft was reported missing the families of the crew were supplied with each other's addresses by the squadron concerned as a result of which they usually established contact with each other.

The information very rarely came complete and so families were left to clutch at straws as bits and pieces of news trickled through from either the Air Ministry or the Red Cross. Any news was immediately shared out, sometimes with joy, sometimes with despair. The delay in information filtering through was at times inexplicable as witnessed in my own case where, even though my whereabouts and safety must have been known early on and I was under the wing of British Intelligence in Paris on the 13th September, I arrived back home on the night of 15th September without any notification being sent to my family.

The following correspondence shows something of the suffering families endured.

76/68/ 195 /P.1.

No. 76 Squadron,   R.A.F. Stn.
Holme on Spalding Moor. Yorks.

23rd. April 1944.

Dear Mrs. Wingham,

It was with the utmost regret that I had to telegraph you that your son, Flying Officer Sydney Thomas Wingham, failed to return from an operational flight against the enemy last night.   He and his crew were detailed to attack the important target of Dusseldorf.

I was impressed by your son's keeness and enthusiasm for his job, right from the time he arrived on the Squadron. This first impression was further strengthened later on by his unquestioned ability as a Bomb Aimer, and his strong sense of duty both in the air and on the ground.   His loss has been received with the greatest sorrow by everyone.

It is desired to explain that the request in the telegram notifying you of the casualty to your son was included with the object of avoiding his chance of escape being prejudiced by undue publicity in case he was still at large.   This is not to say that any information about him is available, but is a precaution adopted in the case of all personnel reported missing.

His personal effects have been carefully collected and forwarded to the R.A.F. Central Depository, Colnebrooke, Slough, Bucks., who will communicate with you in due course regarding disposal.

I am enclosing a list of names and addresses of the next of kin of the crew, in case you might wish to write them.

Please accept on behalf of myself and the entire Squadron, my sincerest sympathy in these anxious days of waiting.

Yours very sincerely,

Wing Commander, Commanding
No. 76 Squadron.   R. A. F.

Mrs. L. Wingham,
42, Croham Park Avenue,
South Croydon,
SURREY.

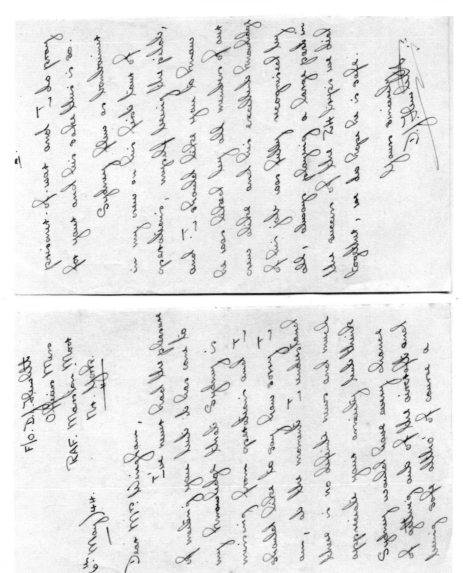

June 14th/44   10 Trenice Terrace,
S. Dennis
Cornwall

Dear Mrs Bingham,

I am writing you to let you know
we had a glad surprise
yesterday, a letter from your
boy at last – he's in a hospital
in Holland with a broken knee
after baling out. He didn't
mention any of the crew except
Flying Officer Stephens, who is
in the hospital with him,
maybe they were the only ones
hurt. I'm hoping you have
also heard from your boy
by now. The letter took 5 weeks
to reach us, so if you haven't
already heard you should do
any day. Wishing you and your
boy all the best –

I am yours very sincerely
Ellen Rowe

2 The Polygon
Eccles
Manchester
Lanc.

Monday

Dear Mrs Wingham,

I am writing to tell you that I have just received a letter card written by my husband F/O Stephen He says he is fit and well but he doesn't mention any of the crew but I am praying that you too have heard something the same as I. This is all I can tell you at present so I will close

Yours Truly.
Mrs Violet Stephen

2 The Polygon
Eccles.

Saturday 15th.   Manchester
                                      Lancs
          My dear Mrs Wingham. —
      I am so sorry. to tell you that
I have no news of F/O Wingham, as.
I have only received one letter from
my husband, but should I hear
anything I will immediately let
you know. I am also sorry that
I have not been able to answer
your letter before now, but you
see I have just arrived home
after a fortnight in a Maternity
Home.
          I am yours Sincerely.
              Mrs Violet Stephen

9. Pineapple Grove
Stirchley. B'ham.

July 5'

Dear Mrs Camelus,

I have just received a
wire from the Air Ministry
to say that from information
received from the Red Cross
my son F/Sgt. H.R. Poole
is believed to have lost
his life, I do hope your
news will be better

Yours Sincerely
Thomas H Poole

TELEPHONE: GERRARD 9234

Extn.................

Any communications on the
subject of this letter should
be addressed to :—

THE
UNDER SECRETARY
OF STATE,

and the following number
quoted :—

Your Ref. ..P.416226/44/P.4.Cas. B4.

AIR MINISTRY

(Casualty Branch),

73-77, OXFORD STREET,

W.1.

7 July 1944.

Madam,

I am directed to refer to the letter dated 3rd May 1944, from the Department notifying you that your son, Flying Officer Sidney Thomas Wingham, Royal Air Force, was reported missing as the result of air operations on the night of the 22nd/23rd April 1944, and to inform you with regret that although no definite news of your son has come to hand, a report regarding certain of the occupants of the aircraft has been received from the International Red Cross.

This report, quoting German information states that Flying Officer S.W.Stephen and Warrant Officer F.L.Rowe were captured on the 23rd April 1944, and Flight Sergeant H.R.Poole, Acting Squadron Leader S.A.Somercales D.F.C., and one member whose identity the German Authorities are unable to establish at present all belonging to the crew of this Halifax aircraft lost their lives on that date.

As there were seven members in the crew it will be appreciated that it is not possible on the above information to state precisely who is the unidentified member, but it is considered that you would wish to be notified of this report.

I am to add an expression of the Department's sympathy with you in your anxiety and to assure you that you will be notified of any further news received.

I am, Madam,
Your obedient Servant,

F. Parkinson

for Director of Personal Services.

Mrs. L.Wingham,
Cambrai, Station Road,
Crawley, Sussex.

43 Caledon Road
Sherwood.
Nottingham
19th July 1944

Dear Mrs Wingham

You will be very pleased to
know we received a post card
from our son this morning
saying he is a prisoner of war
at Stammlager VI G camp
Germany

We do hope and pray all the
crew are safe and it will not
be long before we have our dear
ones at home again

Yours very sincerely
Mr & Mrs H A Reavill

WAR ORGANISATION
OF THE
BRITISH RED CROSS SOCIETY and ORDER OF ST. JOHN OF JERUSALEM

President :	*Grand Prior :*
HER MAJESTY THE QUEEN	H.R.H. The Duke of Gloucester, k.g.

WOUNDED, MISSING AND RELATIVES DEPARTMENT

Chairman : THE DOWAGER LADY AMPTHILL, C.I., G.B.E.

Telephone No.
SLOANE 9696

In replying please quote reference :
EM/EC/C.12122.

**7 BELGRAVE SQUARE,
LONDON, S.W.I**

3rd August, 1944

Dear Mrs. Wingham,

Thank you for your letter of the
27th July concerning your son, Flying Officer
S.T. Wingham, No. 156389.

We completely understand your feelings
on learning that Flying Officer Reavill is a
prisoner of war which, as you so rightly say,
now leaves only the names of two members of the
crew to which no report has been attached.

We realise how very great your anxiety
must be and assure you that directly information
is received about your son, it will be sent to
you by the Air Ministry, and we will write also.

Everything possible is being done to
obtain news and we ask you to accept our sympathy
in your great anxiety.

Yours sincerely,

Margaret Ampthill

Chairman.

Mrs. L. Wingham,
"Cambrai,"
Crawley, Sussex.

9, Pineapple Grove
Hockley
B'ham
Sept. 16' 44

Dear Mr Camelus

So many thanks
for your nice letter this morning,
May I say how very pleased
we all are here to receive
your good news, as we
know what anxiety any
strain you must have
gone through these
last few months, we
hope they are both well.
We are also very pleased
to know they are going
to visit us, I know
they will both have
their time looked up,
but it is very nice of
them to think of us,

as we feel so unsettled
until we can get to know
something about the last
of our son,
We had a letter from the
Air ministry yesterday to
say that he was buried
at Maastricht Holland.
If possible will you send
a P.c. to say which day
they will be coming as I
should not like to be out
when they come.

Thanking you all
yours very sincerely
Thomas H Poole

WAR ORGANISATION
OF THE
BRITISH RED CROSS SOCIETY and ORDER OF ST. JOHN OF JERUSALEM

| *President:* | *Grand Prior:* |
| HER MAJESTY THE QUEEN | H.R.H. THE DUKE OF GLOUCESTER, K.G. |

WOUNDED, MISSING AND RELATIVES DEPARTMENT

Chairman: THE DOWAGER LADY AMPTHILL, C.I., G.B.E.

Telephone No.
SLOANE 9696

In replying please quote reference: DL/MP
RAF C/12122

7 BELGRAVE SQUARE,
LONDON, S.W.I

22nd September, 1944.

Dear Mrs. Wingham,

Thank you so much for your letter of
19th September, in which you give us such good
news of your son, Flying Officer S.T. Wingham,
No.156389, Royal Air Force *and Flying Officer J. H. Lewis.*

We are delighted to know that they are
both safe in this country and that your great
anxiety has ended with such joy and relief.

Yours sincerely,

Margaret Ampthill.

Chairman.   MP DL

Mrs. Wingham,
"Cambrai",
Crawley, Sussex.

Tel. No.—HOLBORN 3434,
        Ext. 489......
Correspondence on the subject
of this letter should be
addressed to
THE UNDER-SECRETARY
        OF STATE,
AIR MINISTRY,...............
and should quote the reference
A. 797356/45/S.7.D.

Your Ref.........................

AIR MINISTRY,

LONDON, W.C.2.

1st June, 1946.

Sir,

   I am directed to inform you that, on the
recommendation of the Air Officer Commanding-in-Chief,
Bomber Command, the American Authorities have
conferred the Distinguished Flying Cross upon you
in recognition of distinguished service in air
operations.   The award will be promulgated in the
Royal Air Force Supplement to the London Gazette
issued on 14th June, 1946.

   Doubtless you will receive the decoration
from the American Embassy in due course.

                    I am, Sir,
                        Your obedient Servant,

Flight Lieutenant
Flying Officer S.T. Wingham,
           7, St. Johns Terrace,
                London, E.7.

Postscript

The Royal Air Force Escaping Society was formed in 1945 in Paris at the express instruction of Lord Portal, the then Chief of Air Staff. The aims of the society were to maintain contact with helpers (those who gave assistance to downed aircrew), and their families and to give assistance, financial and otherwise, when needed. Membership was open only to those who served within the framework of the RAF and who escaped from captivity or evaded capture as a result of a forced descent while on operations and who reached Allied or neutral territory. All substantiated helpers were deemed honorary members.

When the society was formed it was anticipated that, in the light of 1945 life expectations, it would close down in 1985 but when that date arrived it was found that there were still 650 members and around 3,000 helpers still looking to the society.

An extention of five years was made at the 1985 AGM, and then in 1990, it was agreed that, with the numbers still alive, the society should not close down until 1995. In the intervening years, the society arranged for the RAF Benevolent Fund to take over and administer the RAF Escaping Society Charitable Fund at the behest of the RAFES Trustees until the year 2000.

By 1995 these arrangements were in place and the society formally wound up that year with its Standard being laid up in Lincoln Cathedral. And so, for fifty years the RAF men who escaped and evaded capture formally acknowledged their debt to those who risked their lives on their behalf to get them to safety. Christmas cards were sent every year and grants given on a regular basis to those in need. In many cases the friendships have continued with the families and, in 1995, a loose association was formed to maintain contact between members which continued for about ten years. Finally, as agreed, the RAFES Charitable Fund was wound up and disbursed at the turn of the millennium in 2000, details of which are given at the end.

This, however, was not the end of the story. In the late 1980s, Roger Stanton left the army and, being posted to Reserve, found himself in charge of training for escape and evasion. This was something entirely new to him so he contacted the RAFES in London. Seeing the work they carried out on the Continent, he decided to help raise funds for the society. To do this he arranged a sponsored walk by service personnel covering the route used by the Comète escape line from Brussels to the Pyrenees. This was carried out in 1989 and raised about £7,000.

Roger continued with this co-operation with the RAFES throughout the 90s, mounting a number of sponsored walks, and exploring other escape routes in Italy and Greece which had been used by air force and army personnel. At the same time, Eden Camp, near Malton in Yorkshire, an old wartime POW camp, had been opened up as a museum with each hut devoted to a single theme. With a number of army and other friends and the backing of the owner, Mr Stan Johnson, Roger was able to convert one of the huts with an escape and evasion theme. Here many stories may be found of airmen and others who got away, as well as the story of the Great Escape.

In 2003, Roger Stanton, with his group of friends, formally inaugurated the first AGM of the Escape Lines Memorial Society (ELMS). Into this they drew the remnants of the RAFES and also the army escapers and evaders of which there were many, particularly in the Italian theatre. The object of the society is to perpetuate the memory of all those brave people throughout Europe who assisted members of the armed forces to evade capture and reach safety during the Second World War. Also to maintain the routes followed to reach safety.

Each year, in conjunction with local committees, walks are organised of about three days, some difficult, some moderate, covering the freedom trails traversed by service personnel during the war in various parts of the Continent. Areas covered include Arnhem, Sulmona (Italy), Crete, Ruffec (France), Brittany coast, Andorra (France), St. Girons (France and Spain), Poland and Slovakia, Bidassoa (France and Spain) and others.

ELMS membership is open to all who wish to remember and perpetuate the memory of those who helped thousands of Allied servicemen to reach home and safety during the Second World War. It was a very dangerous occupation. A great amount of German effort was exerted to counter the groups involved. It has been calculated that for every member of the Allied forces who reached safety, three helpers were imprisoned or shot. At Eden Camp a memorial has been erected to the helpers consisting of a large rock brought from the Pyrenees combined with a large block of York stone.

ELMS provides the opportunity to recognize and commemorate the work done by those brave people, to meet up with the families of those who helped and to understand the toughness of the terrain that had to be covered. Details of ELMS may be obtained through the Eden Camp Museum near Malton, Yorkshire or via their website; www.escapelines.com.

Dispersal of the RAF Escaping Society Charitable Fund

Terminal grants to helpers (42 x £1500)	£63,000.00
Union Nationale des Evades de Guerre	£5,000.00
Ligne Comète	£10,000.00
Netherlands Escape Lines	£5,314.00
Moate San Marino Trust	£5,000.00
Air Bridge (Charity for Polish & Czech Airmen)	£5,000.00
Papua New Guinea School	£10,000.00
Comset Vol	£2,000.00
St. Clements Dane Church	£5,000.00
Sussex Down RAFA Home	£20,000.00
RAF Benevolent Fund	£11,225.00
	£141,625.00

Index

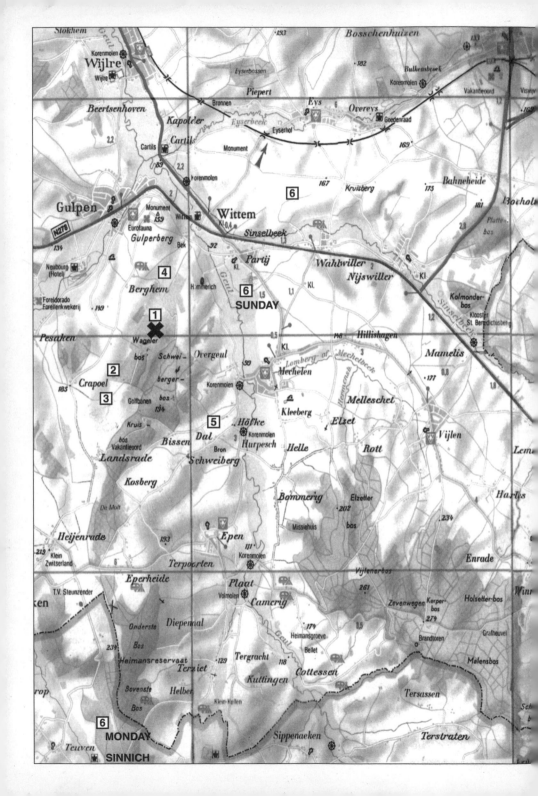